A very personal account

D1341002

YOBS ON THE DOORSTEP

DOORSTEP

Linda Walker

Linda Walker

Yobs on the Doorstep

Copyright © Linda Walker, 2008

Published by Guardian Angels Publications
Yobs on the Doorstep
PO BOX 213
MANCHESTER
M41 4AA

ISBN 978-0-9560098-0-7

Designed and Typeset by Carnegie Book Production, Lancaster
Printed and bound in the UK by CPD, Wales

Contents

Contents

The story

Linda Walker is the teacher who was jailed for going out to some youths with an air pistol. In a distraught state she had vulnerably sought to resolve what the police had been unable to assist her with, protecting her home and family after two years of escalating crime and vandalism, which she perceived threatened the safety of her family in particular the safety of her sons.

She knew she would be in trouble, but thought that somehow her foolish and inappropriate actions would bring the situation to a head and it would be resolved. It was, she was sentenced to six months in prison and the crimes against her family largely not investigated.

The serious charges could have earned her ten years.

Thankfully either the youths concerned eventually showed some decency or whether because their identity was now known the campaign against her family ceased.

The night of the incident had been an exciting 'buzz' for them – it was funny to see her getting into trouble rather than them for a change.

Even they never dreamed she would be treated so harshly, especially for a first offence.

She believes they didn't voluntarily testify against her but were coerced.

The public reaction sympathy and ensuing campaign for her release was unprecedented in recent years. The police complained of receiving hate mail in sacks.

Many politicians including the prime minister were drawn to comment on the case.

She was released on appeal after serving 36 days, her release on the 4th May 2005, the day before the general election, interrupted television programmes to be news flashed across the country.

What did it feel like for Linda?

It was 'amazing'!

This book details her account from the degradation and public humiliation of the trial, her plight in prison to the euphoria of her release.

It could have destroyed her.

Such violent and serious convictions should normally bring a reaction of abhorrence from the public and rightly so, this is not the reaction which Linda receives.

The reaction of the public, the love of her family and the support of her friends gave her the strength to survive.

What has happened to her since and how has it affected her life?

Foreword

I didn't think that anyone in my family would go to prison, but least of all my mum. I had just got home from a night out at my friends house with my fiancé Rob when my brother Craig phoned. He said mum had gone out after some yobs and he was frightened. He said he could hear her shouting up the road and that she and he had both rang the police. We came down straight away, but by then she had been arrested and a group of youths were gathering on the field opposite mum's road. I went onto the field and shouted, "What have you done to my mum?" They seemed to be 'buzzing' about it. My boyfriend Rob got threatened by them. The police were there but they didn't do anything.

Even after she was charged for a firearms charge and affray we didn't think it would go to trial and when it did we didn't think she would be found guilty. It seemed so out of character. The idea that she could go to prison just seemed ridiculous. She has always been a good mum and never done anything to hurt anybody, on the contrary she has done a lot for other people, not only me and my brothers but a lot of other people as well. At the time of the incident we both worked at a special school for children with behavioural problems, I was her support worker. She did a lot of extra things for the children, she felt sorry because a lot of them were very deprived and wanted to compensate for the rotten time that some of them had had. We used to run a Cookery Club after school and took children to Alton Towers quite often as a reward for good behaviour or for an end of term trip. She organised lots of trips for them and we enjoyed getting out of school in the mini-bus.

As we left home to go to court for her sentencing we were all tense. We had sat waiting for her to get ready. She is always last and when we complained she joked and said she had to look glamorous for the cameras, laughing about all the publicity the case had attracted. She has the knack of relieving the tension with her light hearted attitude. In the car we took the mickey out of her partner John's jazz music CD's and I put the radio on and we all sang along to Amarillo. We never thought that she wouldn't be coming home with us. As John said later and like a lot of mums, she is the lynchpin of our family. It was the worst day of my life.

The children at school were very upset. They replaced her with supply teachers at first, but our children don't like strangers and it wasn't very successful. When she was sacked some of the children protested and one stormed in the head teacher's office shouting and kicking the furniture. Another lad got on the roof and refused to come down. It was very upsetting for everyone. I was by then doing mum's Food Technology teaching as an instructor, my qualification is not in teaching. The children accepted me because I was mum's daughter and they knew me. I stayed until all the children mum knew had left and then I left myself as it was a very stressful place to work and I had done five years.

Her case and latterly this book has taken over mum's life since the night of the incident. We just couldn't believe the massive response to her plight. People were just outraged and very upset. Mum was so grateful for the support and understanding – she says it saved her! It spurred her on to fight for her job, against her convictions and to retain her right to teach. She has been obsessed with it and could not move on until she had written it. She felt compelled to let people know just how important their support was to her. Thankfully it is now finished, at last! Mums got a new role coming up now because Rob and I are having a baby!

Donna

Donna and Rob's Wedding – 24th June 2006

Acknowledgement

With thanks to Clarissa Langham without whose help and advice I could not have written this book.

Dedication

This book is dedicated to Gary Dixon, the lad who got on the roof for me, and who, on 4th April, 2008, died of an overdose of methadone, aged 17.

Glossary of Abbreviations

MP	Member of Parliament
DS	Detective Sergeant
IPCC	Independent Police Complaints Commission
GMP	Greater Manchester Police
PW 1	Police Witness 1
PW 2	Police Witness 2
CPS	Criminal Prosecution Service
HMP	Her Majesty's Prison
HDC	Home Detention Curfew
PO	Prison Officer
SPO	Senior Prison Officer
CI	Chief Inspector
ACC	Assistant Chief Constable
RCJ	Royal Courts of Justice
LEA	Local Education Authority
NASUWT	National Association of Schoolmasters and Union of Women Teachers
ET	Employment Tribunal
EAT	Employment Appeal Tribunal
DfES	Department for Education and Skills
CCRC	Criminal Cases Review Commission
GTC	General Teaching Council

PART 1

The Incident

1   A Full Moon and Friday, 13th August

The car boot was packed to the brim with all our holiday essentials. The surface of the car glinted in the early evening sun as I looked out through the lounge window to see John adding the final polish. His car has always been his prized possession, in fact he and my son James are both mad about cars. I watched him fondly as he started to clear up his cleaning equipment, absorbed in the job. Then he sensed I was watching him and turned to smile his kind smile at me. Calm moments like this, moments of normality, were rare and precious to us. During the last two years we had become victims in our own home.

I walked through the lounge into the kitchen, where I was preparing one of our favourite meals. The house was spotless; it always had to be that way before we went away. I was and still am very house-proud anyway. I was never happier than in the spacious living kitchen of our detached house, with John, my twin sons Craig and James or daughter Donna wandering in for a chat. I had always wanted a domesticated life, ever since I was little. My mum and dad would tease me about how I would love to put on a romantic dinner party for them, enlisting my little brother as a fellow waiter. It was no surprise to anyone when I decided to train to be a cookery teacher. As well as being a career which I would love, I knew it would fit in well with children and I always wanted to be a mum. More than that, I wanted to be a good mum.

John traipsed back into the house as I stirred the chicken korma.

"Do you want a glass of wine?" I asked.

"Go on then, we are on holiday!" he said. He kissed me and smiled. I felt a wave of relief to see him relaxed. For a long time I had been worried about John's health, more even than my own even though that had suffered as well. He had been referred to the hospital with chest pains and while we were relieved when tests for heart problems proved negative, the realisation that they were caused by stress was shocking. He has such a tolerant, gentle nature, that it did not seem fair. He had even been forced to take some time off from his job as a Head of Motor Vehicle Studies at the college where he worked. Now at least though, it was the school holidays and John was clearly starting to wind down. I felt optimistic for the first time in months.

My sons James and Craig still lived with us while Donna had moved out to live with her fiancé Rob not far away from where we lived in Urmston, Manchester. James had gone out with his girlfriend in Craig's car that night. He had just passed his test that day and was very pleased with himself. A few months earlier he had bought a car to do up as a project. He was keeping it on the drive while he and John worked on it so Craig was allowing him to use his car until it was finished. I served up the tea for John, Craig and myself, and after the meal we all sat down to watch a film on television. Craig got up to make a cup of tea for us.

"Mum, why is there a gallon container on top of James' car?" he shouted to me.

With those few words my sense of relaxation dissolved. I snapped to attention, every muscle in body tensing up in anticipation of what was coming next. John and I looked at each other. A dark expression crossed his face and I knew he felt the same way as I did. I got up first and John followed me into the kitchen. Sure enough, a gallon container which I had rinsed out to take with us to the caravan for water was on top of James' car. What's more, it was face down with the contents poured over the roof.

"Anything could have been in that container!" I said. It had only had water inside but it could have been anything: cleaning fluids, bleach ... As I thought of the damage it could have caused to my son's car I felt anger bubbling up inside me.

"Leave it Linda," John said wearily. "They're probably miles away by now." I went out through the back door and the water was still dripping off the car. "If they are that near, I'm going to find out who they are and then I'm going to call the police and get this stopped." I thought to myself.

I started walking down the road: I was hardly dressed for a pursuit, wearing diamante flip-flops on my feet, but I had no time to waste. Our house is at the end of a cul-de-sac off a fairly busy road. The cul-de-sac was deserted so I walked quickly to the junction with Flixton Road and looked along it to the left and right. There was no-one around at all apart from two youths a hundred yards or so to the left, walking away from the entrance to our road. I looked again, but there was no-one else at all, even though I had a good view for some way along the road in both directions. It had to be these two youths but I had no proof. I decided to follow them at a distance. Craig had walked in the other direction.

It was a warm evening and I looked up and saw a full moon. It was also Friday the 13th and I would later reflect on the irony of this 'unlucky' date. The youths I was following had no idea I was there as they were so wrapped up in their conversation. Both were wearing dark clothing, one wore a hooded top pulled over his face and both wore jogging pant bottoms. They crossed over to the other side of the road, where a warning sign had been put to warn pedestrians about some council road repairs underway on the pavement. They lifted the road sign and took it into the middle of the road. I watched as they deliberately lined it up in the centre of the lane, turning it side-on so that it would not be easily seen by oncoming cars. Then, they calmly walked back to my side of the road and stood back under some trees, folded their arms, and watched the road. I realised with horror that they were waiting for a car to hit the sign on the tree lined road.

I simply could not believe what I was seeing. As a teacher at a special school for teenagers with emotional difficulties and challenging behaviour, I was by no means naïve about the kind of activities some young people got up to on Friday nights. This, though, was nothing but downright dangerous and malicious. These boys were out looking for trouble and I now knew for sure that they were the ones who had been at our house minutes earlier. My first priority now though was to move the sign from the road to prevent an accident. I checked for traffic and quickly ran across the road and threw it onto the pavement, still keeping an eye on the youths. As they saw what I was doing, they started to wander off nonchalantly. They then turned and came back to the road from the other direction, as if they had been coming in the other direction all along. They obviously did not know that I had been watching them.

As I walked towards them, one of the boys ran away. I stood in front of the remaining youth, who looked around 18 years old and was the one without the hooded top. I could feel the anger bubbling up inside me.

"Are you a psycho?" I shouted at him. The sound would not seem to come out properly because I was too angry, my voice was shaking. "What do you think you're doing putting a sign into the road, for cars to hit? Are you trying to cause an accident? Are you trying to kill someone?"

"I didn't put a sign in the road," he said. He was arrogant and cocky and looked straight at me as he said this blatant lie, even though I had seen him doing just that.

"Are you a psycho?" I found myself shouting again. I couldn't believe that he was denying something I had clearly seen with my own eyes. He looked annoyed then and started walking off. I was not going to let him off that lightly, I wanted answers. I wanted to confront him about being at our house before he ran away like his friend so I followed him across the road.

"Don't come to our house again," I said, wanting to see his reaction. Again, he ignored me. I realised that I needed to say something dramatic to get his attention.

"Don't come to my house again because if you do, I've got guns." I said. It worked. He stopped and turned to look at me.

"Oooooh she's got guns," he said in a mocking tone. We were now standing alongside the football field, about 250 yards from our home. I could hear giggling from behind a wall next to the field and I realised that other youths, perhaps including the one who was with him earlier, were listening.

"Go and get your guns then, go and get your shotgun," he said. Now he had an audience.

"It's not a shotgun actually, it's an air rifle," I said, casually, not wanting to lose his attention now I had it and not wanting to lose face. It was not a lie. My son James had an air rifle and as a result of the escalating attacks on our home, I also kept an air pistol in our bedroom for protection in case of a burglary. It made me feel safer.

Another youth stepped out from behind the wall. He did not speak but his manner was aggressive and threatening and he squared up to me with his legs apart, chest and shoulders out, forearms raised slightly and fists clenched. The other youth now did the same, bolstered by his friend's presence. What a pair of cowards, I thought. Why was this other lad getting involved, had he been to the house too? As if to answer me, the youths behind the wall then started to sing: "Linda and John, Linda and John" tauntingly. I couldn't believe they were being so flagrant. They obviously thought they were above the law. They weren't scared of me, they just thought I was some stupid woman who couldn't do anything to them. I now knew for sure that they were connected to the attacks on our house and I was not going to lose face and allow it to continue and perhaps get even worse.

As they stood in front of me, I made a decision that would come back to haunt me. I thought of the worst thing I could possibly say to give them a shock. They would probably not know where I worked and it was the last thing they would be expecting from a middle class, middle aged woman. They would have to take me seriously, they would know I was not scared of them. I curled my lip and looked them up and down.

I said: "You f****** fat, ugly c***".

They just stood there looking at me, aggressive and arrogant, so I repeated: "If you come to my house, I've got guns." The youths behind the wall laughed and taunted.

"Go and get your guns then," they said. They were not frightened at all, they thought I was a joke. They knew I would not actually get the guns. Or would I? The thought popped into my head like a light bulb switching on. They thought I would go quietly back to the house and they would stay out there, laughing about me, probably telling their friends. Had I done enough to stop them coming to the house? I knew I had not. Had I made it worse? Possibly. The idea flashed brighter. I was going to do it. Then they would know I was serious. What did I have to lose? I really didn't care any more.

"Right then, I will." I said. I turned and walked back towards the house to get the guns.

2   That's an Arrestable Offence

I walked back into the kitchen, where the dishes from our lovely, relaxed, meal were stacked up next to the dishwasher. John was nowhere to be seen.

"Charming," I thought, "He's obviously worried about me."

I had assumed he would have come to check I was alright but evidently he had better things to do. He wasn't even waiting for me in the lounge. I stomped upstairs loudly and found him messing around with some of his electrical equipment in our bedroom.

"Thanks for coming to look for me," I said sarcastically, without stopping to talk to him. I knew what I was going to do and I didn't want to waste any more time. It was blatantly obvious that if this problem was going to be sorted out, I was going to have to do it.

I went into James' bedroom and got his air-rifle from down the side of his wardrobe. I knew exactly where it was because I was the one who cleaned the house. James' dad, my ex husband, had bought the gun as a Christmas present about two years earlier. I wasn't that keen but it was only for target practice and it was just an air rifle, which most young lads tend to go through a phase of owning. As it turned out he only used it for a while and when he ran out of pellets, he didn't bother to get any more. Now, with this rifle in my hand, I stomped across the landing into our bedroom to get the air pistol. John had bought this about a year previously to scare away squirrels which had invaded the loft and repeatedly chewed through wiring and cut off the television reception.

"I've got the rifle. Where's the air pistol?" I shouted to John in a purposefully matter-of-fact tone. This will shock him, I thought. I knew full well where it was. I took this in my other hand and stomped loudly out onto the landing. It felt ridiculous. Here I was, a middle-aged, middle-class teacher, holding two air guns in my hands and preparing to go out on the street.

There was one vital thing which I needed to do first. I had known I would do it from the moment the lightbulb had flickered to life inside my head. I was going to call the police. This was vital if my plan was going to work. The two things were completely intertwined, one could not be contemplated without the other. It just wouldn't work.

"Is it loaded?" I asked John, who had now come out into the landing.

"Yes Linda, it's loaded," he answered in a weary tone. He was humouring me. He wasn't taking me seriously either, just like the youths. I'll show him, I thought. I tried to fire the air pistol at the ceiling but it didn't work.

"How do you turn it on?" I asked. John calmly flicked the safety switch off and looked at me with his eyebrows raised. He thought I would calm down and return to normal in a minute. This made me even angrier. I stomped off and started down the stairs. Then, to shock him even more, I turned around and fired the gun on the stairs. It went off. I thought: "That will get him worried, not coming out to protect me!" Craig was standing at the top of the stairs and looking at me as though I was mad.

I fired it again, in the other direction from where Craig was standing. Then I stomped off down the stairs.

At this point, John realised I was serious.

"Don't go out again Linda. It might not be them," he said.

"It is them. They're singing "Linda and John" at me," I shouted. This seemed to change his attitude. No-one except our immediate neighbours knew us that well in Flixton, our friends lived in different parts of Greater Manchester.

"Phone the police," he said then.

"I am phoning the police, that's what I've come down to do!" I shouted back. I walked into the kitchen and dialled 999. John walked past me and out through the back door.

The operator answered and I immediately gave my name and address.

"What's the problem there?" she said.

"I'm going over to that field over the road, I've got an air rifle and a pistol and I'm going to shoot the fucking vandals who keep coming round here ..." The operator interrupted me.

"Right, number one ..." I wasn't going to be interrupted.

"Come round here, damaging my house and my property ..." She interrupted again.

"Number one, don't need that language, number two you don't make threats like that on a taped line."

I said: "I'm sorry, but ..." She didn't give me a chance to finish.

"You're going to be arrested," she said. I continued what I had planned to say.

"I'm going to the fields on Flixton Road and I've got a pistol and I've got an air rifle and I'm going to shoot them."

"Then you're going to be arrested."

"The psychos have just put a road sign in the middle of the road, side on, for a car to hit it."

"I do realise that and I realise you're distressed but you can't threaten people ..."

"They've got nothing themselves but they want to damage other people's property and I'm on my way now. I'm just telling you."

"Fair enough. OK. Goodbye. I'm going to terminate the call now." I couldn't quite believe that she wasn't trying to keep me on the phone when I was making these threats. She seemed more interested in displaying her knowledge of the law.

"I'm on my way with me weapons shooting people." I suppose I wanted her to tell me not to do it and to give me some reassurance that the police were on their way.

"I'm going to have to terminate the call because you've made a threat with a firearm which is a very serious offence," she said.

"I'm going over there now and I'm going to do it," I said.

"Right that's an arrestable offence, goodbye," she said, and hung up.

So that was it. What other choice did I have now? The police had not helped me so far and I was not prepared to back down and continue being a victim. I opened the back door and went out onto the street with the air rifle and pistol. I could see myself doing it, it was like an 'out of body experience,' and I thought how bizarre my behaviour was but I wanted to be extreme. Craig had been hovering behind me while I made the phone call and tried to follow me.

"Don't you come out, get back inside and look after the house!" I shouted. I was very dismissive but it was because I didn't want to get him involved. In recent weeks Craig had borne the brunt of the long-term victimisation we had been suffering. He had been struggling with his sexuality for some time and we had received a string of abusive and threatening

13

phone calls making reference to this. John and I had answered the phone on both occasions and had been threatened along with Craig. We felt sure that it must be linked to the attacks on our home. It had all been going on for too long and this was just the latest development. I had long suspected that those responsible might know the boys and that it could be a form of bullying. The last thing I wanted was to put Craig in line for direct abuse.

As I walked onto Flixton Road again, I expected to see flashing police lights and hear sirens. The street was silent. I still wore my diamante flip flops on my feet but now I was armed. How ridiculous I must have looked. As I approached the youths I heard them giggling and shouting: "Hear she comes!" This was obviously the best night's entertainment they'd had for a long time. As I drew nearer they all dispersed except the one I had initially spoken to. I looked around for John but couldn't see him. I was on my own with him.

He said: "Ooh, here she comes with her guns. Go on, shoot me." I stopped about ten yards away from him, just close enough for him to get a good look at the guns. As he looked I glanced down the street but there was no sign of the police.

The youth looked me over as if I wasn't worth his time. He nonchalantly crossed over to the other side of the road where his friends were, so I followed him. Then he drew near to me again. He had been drinking and he was so near that I could smell alcohol on his breath.

"Go on then, shoot me you silly old woman," he said. He was so near now that I worried he might try to grab the pistol but I knew that if I backed off I would lose face. As if to reinforce this, he slowly moved his right foot right up against mine. Toe to toe.

"Move your foot," I said. He didn't. I pointed the gun at his foot. Still he didn't move. I obviously wasn't going to shoot him so I moved it to the side of his foot and shot it at the pavement. It was as if to say: "I could have done it, but I didn't." The gun made a pathetic puff. I looked down the road to see if there were any signs of the police. The only people I could see were the other youths peeping at us from a doorway.

I had his attention now so I fired the gun twice more at the tarmac away from us. The youth didn't seem frightened, he was more aggressive if anything.

"You can't walk around with guns, I'm phoning the police," he said, waving his mobile phone.

"I already have and you'll be in trouble when they arrive. They'll want to talk to you about what's been going on at our house and putting that road sign in the road for people to hit." I could see John out of the corner of my eye and felt a wave of relief.

"You're the one who'll be in trouble," he said.

John arrived and said: "What's your mobile number?" He had seen him waving his mobile at me. We had recorded the mobile number which has been used to make the threatening phone calls. He refused to give his number and denied being involved in any calls.

Suddenly, a black Astra pulled up. Two men got out of the car. I thought: "They could be thugs who the youths have phoned."

"Police, put your weapons on the ground," they said. At last, they were here.

"You're under arrest," one of the officers said, and starting reading my rights.

"But it's them who should be under arrest, they ..." I tried to explain about the attacks on our house and the road sign but I was not allowed to say anything. A police van arrived and as I protested I was briskly escorted into it. I didn't know what to say.

"I'm going to contact my MP," I heard myself saying. It must have sounded ridiculous.

Inside the van there was a black, metal cage. I was told to get inside it and sit on a bench. The policeman slid the mesh door across and locked it shut. I tried to see what was happening to John but the doors to the van were closed. I thought: "John will tell the police what really happened and everything will be alright. At least now we'll get a chance to tell the full story and have someone listen to us and question those responsible. Nothing can be worse that what we've been through already." The van then lurched off for the police station.

3 The Criminal and the Witnesses

It was now 4 p.m. the next day and I was in a police cell. I had hardly had any sleep at all. After being booked in at around 1 a.m. I'd initially been told I would be interviewed in around 20 minutes. The custody sergeant had later come to say that there had been a fatal road accident, which meant the interview would be delayed. They had at least allowed me to ring John, who sounded stressed, but it was good to hear his voice. The 'bed' was a concrete slab with a plastic coated pad stretched over it but I managed to doze through sheer exhaustion. As I fell in and out sleep, thoughts of what had happened the night before and during the previous two years swirled through my mind.

It was the summer of 2002 when the first attack happened: John hates flying so we had bought a new caravan and put it on a site in the rolling hills of North Wales where we would go for weekends and during the school holidays. We returned from a lovely break during Whit Week to find that twelve fish including some beautiful and valuable koi carp had been stolen from the pond in our back garden. To our dismay we found scrape marks all around the pond where it appeared that someone had dragged a net around to fish them out. We were upset but put it down to a one-off prank by children. Then in June, tyres were stolen from the garden and a brush thrown into our hedge. We had some lovely garden ornaments and these went missing in July. As if this wasn't bad enough, we found some thrown and smashed in the road. They hadn't even wanted them for themselves. In August, we found dents in the back door where it had been kicked and eventually it had to be replaced at a cost of £900.

It was a hard time in many ways. John had recently moved in with us after a difficult start to our relationship. We had both known each other as work colleagues for many years and I think we had been attracted to each other for some time. My marriage was not working out and John eventually confided in me that the same was true for his. We started to have an affair. It was strange for both of us, we could hardly believe we were involved in such a potentially scandalous and damaging situation, but that was what happened. We wanted to be together and after a while we decided we had to come out into the open. We both felt very guilty but I knew that it would be better for everyone to be honest and say my marriage wasn't working and that I had met someone I loved. My husband and John's wife both reacted badly and my children were still at junior school so it was difficult for them. I tried to support them and after a while things seemed to settle down. Four years later, we had finally reached the point where they were willing to accept John moving in.

John had two grown-up children of his own and tried to get to know the boys without seeming too pushy. He was not their dad and he did not want to try to be. He would sometimes however, take James off racing remote controlled cars, as they had a shared interest in it. It seemed to be going quite well, then, when these attacks started happening, something changed. John would be very quiet and seemed to be brooding about something. He eventually admitted that he feared it had something to do with the boys, perhaps because they were angry that he had moved in after all. Maybe they didn't want to upset me by openly rejecting him and this was their way of getting revenge? I knew they would not do this because they were my sons. It caused some tension between us. I understood his feelings and didn't want to take sides but my mothering instincts were so strong that I had to defend my boys.

The attacks eased off after the school holidays and then in November two police officers came to the house to speak to James. There had been a break-in at the school tuck shop and they suspected someone he knew at school. James had heard about the incident but didn't want to give a statement for fear of reprisals. However, they did manage to prosecute two youths who were responsible. On Christmas Day, John's car window was smashed. We reported this to the police. We still didn't know if it was connected to the other incidents or to James' visit from the police. We felt uneasy.

In May, again during the school holidays, our front door was split, as though it had been kicked. During the next few months a motion sensor lantern at the front door was smashed, a case of beer stolen from a table in our back garden and our two sheds broken into. In July the police caught two of four youths running away from the house at 3 a.m., when they ran out in front of a police van on Flixton Road. James had fitted an alarm in his shed (the one in which he kept his fishing tackle). We hoped the incidents would stop but they didn't. A fish feeder which John's son had bought him as a Father's Day present was vandalized and knocked into the pond, a second security light was smashed with a brick, and then a youth ran into our back garden one Saturday night. I was washing up in the kitchen when a newly installed security light flashed on. He looked very startled and ran away. Then at Easter 2004 when we went away to the caravan the boys didn't want to come, but they seemed not to want to stay at home either. Craig went to stay at a friends and James went fishing on Sale Marina for a few days. When they returned home our shed had been burgled again. My daughter and her fiancé, Rob, were with us at the caravan when James rang to tell me what had happened. That brought us up to the recent school summer holiday. The mirrors and rear windscreen wiper on Craig's car were pulled off and the windscreen hit with a brick. Days later we had the offensive phone calls for Craig. I went over the incidents as I lay in the cell. I felt sorry for what I had done but surely the police would realise why I had acted as I did once I told them all about the background.

At around 7 a.m. a Detective Sergeant (DS) came into the cell. They were going to search my house and he wanted to know if there were any other weapons there. I confirmed there weren't. I tried to explain the background but he wasn't interested. I would get my chance to make a statement at the interview, he said. I was eventually shown into the interview room with my solicitor. I had initially declined legal advice. Why did I need a solicitor when I was just going to tell the truth? When I told the duty officer this he encouraged me to accept a solicitor so I decided to take his advice. Having listened to the tape of my call, the solicitor said he was concerned and advised me not to say anything at this stage.

"Say nothing? I've been waiting for this chance for ages. I am going to tell them exactly what has been happening." If I didn't, I might have well have stayed inside. I would have been safely at home now if so and so would John. What upset me most was that they had now also arrested John and interviewed him.

The DS asked me to explain the events leading up to my arrest. I hardly knew where to start. I said: "There is a whole series of events that led up to it. Last Sunday and Monday I had nuisance phone calls and reported it to the police. This is being investigated. I've got two boys, twins 17 – James and Craig. They were calling Craig a "poof" and saying: "Does he want bumming?" Then when John answered later they said: "Is Craig in? Can I leave him a message? Tell him does he want bumming?" John said: "Well what if I don't?" "Well you'll get bummed as well" they said."

I told him about all the incidents. It felt a relief to have someone listening to this at last. I continued: "So it's been going on one thing after another, vandalism at the house and since my boys have bought cars then they've started to pick on those. What happened last night, I'd got a big gallon of washing up liquid ..." The DS lifted up the empty bottle and interrupted.

"Can I just take you back a bit because you're saying that they were the ones that were doing the vandalising. You're sat in your living room aren't you? You can't say they are the ones that are vandalising because you haven't seen them do it, have you?" he said.

"No, I haven't seen them but I know damn well ..." I said.

"No, you're making an assumption."

"OK, I saw them put the sign in the road ..." I said.

"That's not vandalising your children's stuff, as you say. You're making a very broad range assumption aren't you?" he asked.

"Well, there was nobody else around. I went out walking around, and it had only just happened because there was still water on the car."

"Yes but what was the temperature like at that time of night?"

"It was quite warm because I was walking around."

"If someone poured water on that it could be there for a while."

"Well it only took as long as it took them to get up the road to the bus stop." I said.

He replied: "You didn't see them do anything to your son's car did you?"

"No I can't prove it."

"I know for a fact that John didn't see anybody and I know your son didn't see anyone," he said, referring to the fact that he had interviewed John.

"But I saw them put the sign in the road, so that shows what type of person they are."

He questioned our claim that we had been targeted personally over the previous two years. "We've researched our systems today and we've found three incidents at your house that's all," he said

"In the last few weeks."

"We've found the burglary of your shed in April. You weren't the only person to have their shed broken into in that area at that time, so that's clearly not personally targeted at you."

"Yes ..." I said.

"Then you've got the damage to the motor vehicle on the 1st of this month, where the mirrors were broken and then you've got the phone calls, now I'll grant you the phone calls were making comments about your son."

"These lads knew our name, did I say that?"

"We know that but what I'm saying is the only one that we can see that has a definite personal connection is the phone calls and that's being investigated by the police."

How did they know that there wasn't a personal connection if they weren't going to investigate it? Was it all just a coincidence that we had been targeted so many times then?

"What about this incident last night, coming into my garden and taking the bottle and putting it on my son's car?" I said.

"There was no damage caused to your son's car, a plastic bottle had been placed on top."

"They didn't know that that was water."

"It's a washing up liquid bottle."

"It was dark, it could have been anti-freeze."

"What security arrangements have you got at the back of your house?"

"I've got a gate that I paid £700 for. I lock it with a padlock which I put on when I go to bed. Also I've got lights that come on but you have got to get right to the back for the lights to come on and they didn't get that far."

"There is a lime green label on the bottle, there are street lamps. There's no way on earth that anybody is going to confuse that with a bottle of anti-freeze."

"They didn't know it was water."

"But you knew it was water though didn't you, so you knew that there was no damage to James' car other than having water on it."

"They had been in my garden again, they had stolen. I know that it's only a plastic washing up bottle – but they shouldn't come up my path and take my things and pour it on my son's car."

It was clear that he was not interested in finding out whether these youths were responsible. He only wanted to reinforce the case against me.

"You're making an assumption aren't you?"

"Based on how they were behaving when I went down the road and when I saw them trying to cause an accident by putting the sign in the road," I said.

"Even so, you're making that assumption, and there has been no damage caused to your son's property."

"Not that time no. Not on this occasion no, but they've been up my path, taking our things and interfering with our property."

"You don't know that."

"Well someone has."

"It might have been James."

"James was out in the car."

"It could be a neighbour, it could be anyone."

"No, my neighbours aren't so cheeky to come up our path. I accept that I've assumed, but I've based that assumption on pretty strong evidence when I saw how they behaved on the road."

I then discovered that they had taken a statement from one of the youths but not as a suspect, rather as a witness for the police!

He said: "This offence under the firearms act Section 16A could potentially get you ten years in prison." Ten years? Well that was obviously ridiculous, he was just trying to frighten me now to get me to say what he wanted to hear, but I had had enough of him as well by then, so I answered, "Well I could do with a rest!" I knew I had done wrong and I felt sorry about that. I fully accepted that I had to face the consequences, but ten years for a firearm offence? I hadn't injured anyone. It wasn't even a real gun.

He said: "You are an experienced teacher that deals with problematic children that is used to dealing with confrontation."

"But it doesn't mean they don't get you any less mad, it's different at work."

"What would have happened ..." I knew what he was going to say.

"I'm in a professional capacity at work, when I'm at home I'm a mum and if someone attacks your own family it makes you very distressed."

"How would Craig would have felt if he had been walking down the road at 12.45 a.m. and was confronted by a woman armed with two guns?" he said.

"Frightened to death probably, but he, this youth, wasn't frightened. He didn't even walk off."

"He was frightened when you shot at him."

"Good. I didn't shoot at him anyway, I shot the road. He'd have been frightened if he'd have been in a car and hit that sign he put in the road wouldn't he?"

"I think we've covered what you've done," he said, seeming satisfied with what I had just said.

I apologised for frightening the police officers who arrived at the scene, but refused to say I was sorry for frightening the youth.

"I can't say I'm sorry I challenged him, no, I'm not sorry. I don't know, I think I needed to do it to get rid of some of my anger because of all the frustration and all the things that have happened."

"This could have ended up a very different outcome."

"I know but the law is on their side all the time, they're protected aren't they."

"That doesn't give you the right to take the law into your own hands."

"Yes I know, yes." I said. I obviously knew what I had done wasn't right.

The interview ended and I was served with a bail notice. I was not to contact the youths who were now police witnesses, I was told. My solicitor kept shaking his head, saying: "I don't think they will charge you, I've never seen anything like this before." John was brought through. He looked awful, very worried and as if he'd had no sleep. He had declined legal advice, thinking it unnecessary because he knew he had not done anything wrong and would only be telling the truth. He was also unhappy about his interview as the police had alleged he had also been holding a gun, which was untrue. I was not worried about this, knowing that John's account would be entirely honest and feeling sure that they would be able to see his true character. We trusted the justice system and had faith that the truth would come out as long as we were honest.

4   My History

I was born on the 11th February, 1957 at Sale Cottage Hospital in Greater Manchester, to mum and dad Margaret and Jim Mairs, very much a wanted child. Mum gave up her job as a machinist, as women did in those days, dad was an area manager for Rentokill. He went to work in suit and had a company car which gave us an apparent air of prosperity although he was not particularly well paid. We were part of a close wider family of grandparents aunties uncles and cousins as both mum and dad were from a family of five. Three years later brother Christopher was born and the family was complete.

When I was five Margaret and Jim decided to leave the rat race, when they bought a milk round in New Mills, Derbyshire, and a new house. I have happy memories of the lovely countryside farms and animals, the snow too, as it was one of the coldest winters on record. I went to Spring Bank Infants School, which for its time was very progressive and I enjoyed learning through lots of practical activities. The countryside, though, was not really a good area in which to buy a milk round, so in 1965 we moved back to Sale. Dad started a taxi business. I attended Limetree School at Sale Moor, and being borderline in my 11+ then went to Norris Road Secondary

School. Here I made lots of friends, many of whom I am proud still to call my friends to this day, such as Barbara who was a character referee for me at the trial and also one of the "Free Linda" campaigners.

I trained as a teacher of Home Economics as it was then, at Elizabeth Gaskell College in Manchester and started my first job when I was 21. It was a lovely job at Worsley College in the 'posh' part of Salford and I loved it so much that I stayed for 23 years. I taught mainly girls aged 16 to 18. They were a great age to teach, full of fun and enthusiasm for life. I remember one time when we went on a study trip. They knew I was a Manchester City fan and as I got onto the minibus, I noticed they had all put on Manchester United shirts. It was like that all the time. I planned lots of visits for them and would always have a party in the last lesson prior to Christmas. At Easter I gave Easter eggs to students who still had 100% attendance and when we finished for the summer we would do a buffet and have some music. I thought it was important that they enjoyed themselves at College and felt like they were part of it.

After a few years, the things I did suddenly became held up as good practice rather than scoffed at as a 'bit of a skive' – getting paid for having fun. Colleges in response to government targets, sought to increase attendance and retention rates and doing social activities kept the students motivated to carry on coming into college. Also College got funding related to the achievements of the students, so if they left before the end of their course they obviously didn't achieve their qualification goal. This was just a bonus for me because I had always included social activities in my programmes of study anyway. It was having that sort of autonomy that made my job so enjoyable.

In 1980 when I was 23 I met Leslie Walker on a night out

with friends at a pub in Sale. In 1982 we married and lived in Sale Moor. We were thrilled and delighted to have a daughter, Donna, in 1984 and the boys a couple of years later. Having the children was lovely although it was hard work when the twins came along. I had three children under three and I still worked full-time because I loved my job so much I didn't want to give it up. The twins were so different from a very young age. It always made me laugh. James was a proper boyish little boy, always into trucks, fishing and the likes, whereas Craig was more interested in going shopping with me or sewing and knitting. Donna's life took on a different purpose once I had the twins, she blossomed into the role of big sister and enjoyed organising and taking charge of everything. We had moved to a bigger house in Flixton before the twins were born.

I had ended up teaching at a college rather than a school by accident but only eventually left because my job became redundant. For my last five years at college I ran a course called Modern Cookery which was for adults. It appealed to a wide range of people, some who were just looking for a new interest whilst others wanted a new career. There were also retired, widowed and divorced people who wanted or needed to learn to cook. A few of the students had special needs some having been referred onto the course to help them with life skills. My students were a very diverse group ranging from people with learning difficulties and disabilities to professionals with degrees and all ages from 15 to 72. But amazingly enough they all got on well, helped each other and enjoyed each others company. Many kept coming back for years to take other or more advanced modules. When one of the students came to presentation night to collect his certificate he came with his wife and wore a black dress suit and bow tie! When our oldest student Ronnie passed all his modules the other students and I did an evening dinner party for him at college and he brought all his family including his grandchildren! It was great for the image of the College in the community. College was like an extension of my family

The course provided therapy for many of the students as much as education. I organised numerous social events. We went on trips to places like Derbyshire, Howarth in Yorkshire, Blackpool and 'shop till you drops' to Cheshire Oaks outlet centre. There was always a loose connection to catering, such as a chip shop lunch with a tour of the potato preparation area, but a large social element of recreation and fun. I had some really lovely students and I am still in contact with some of them. Whilst at the college I always enjoyed the work I did with students with varying degrees of special need and they enjoyed my informal and unconventional approach. I was never a very 'teacherified' person, I relied on my strength as a communicator, my sense of humour and my love of food and cooking.

In 2001 My Modern Cookery course was axed when part time courses were sacrificed to preserve the full time provision for school leavers in a college rationalization process. I chose to take the redundancy package on offer from the college and decided that I would like to work at a special school. I heard about a job at a school for children with social emotional and behavioural difficulties through a colleague of mine whose friend was the Deputy Head. She told me they were looking for a teacher of Food Technology. The job was not available immediately, however, so I spent a term covering for maternity leave for the Head of Food Technology at Bingley Grammar School in Yorkshire working in the highly successful Design and Technology Department.

I enjoyed my time in Yorkshire: the scenery was lovely and

the people very genuine and down to earth. The children were a startling contrast to those who I was to come into contact with when working in Salford. Some of the sixth form pupils came to school driving 4x4s. One of the younger pupils said to me in class one day "I went to the ballet last night Miss, we had our own box." The head gave me a lovely reference for my new job commenting that despite the substantial distance I had to travel, I had never arrived late or left early. I did find 'proper' teaching very monotonous though with massive classes, loads of marking and the report writing! It was too impersonal for me, too much like a conveyor belt.

I started my new job at the special school, Salford, after the Christmas holidays in January 2002. My first day was a staff development day at the Hilton hotel at Manchester airport. The staff was not like the staff at Bingley Grammar. My boss shaved his head, dyed the stubble blonde and wore Dr. Martin boots. They all seemed a bit wacky. When I said I thought it was the kids that were supposed to have behavioral difficulties at this school not the staff, they laughed but it was the manner in which they laughed that was worrying – it was sort of hysterical! Only when I got to know them better did I appreciate how caring and committed they were. They had to be to put up with their pupils!

5   Teaching Children with Problems

The pupils had a range of social behavioural and emotional problems and were taught in classes of a maximum of eight pupils, by a teacher with at least one support worker. The vast majority of pupils came from deprived backgrounds and truancy was a major problem even though most of them were brought to school by taxi. It would be common to only have three or four pupils at a time. I was told that I would have to follow my children from assembly to the classroom. Otherwise, half of them would disappear out of the building before even getting to classroom. They fought with each other and often had to be separated to avoid a confrontation. In their world if someone insults or offends you a show of aggression is almost obligatory. These were children who lived on their wits and responded quickly to situations. Failure to stand up for oneself was seen as a sign of weakness so we were on the lookout for trouble constantly. They would sometimes wreck classrooms, kicking cupboards and throwing chairs across the room. They would sabotage each other's work if you looked away for a minute. By the end of my first day, I wondered how the teachers could call them 'children' at all!

As I began to get to know the pupils and other teachers I

realised that this was not the whole story. Many of the pupils came from dysfunctional families with tragic backgrounds. Very few of our parents worked at all, only a couple full time and several had severe personal problems including alcohol or drug addictions. Some of the children had been abused in a variety of ways by family members or their partners. Some of them took drugs, sometimes they would have to be taken home because they were 'stoned' and a danger to themselves. A lot of the children drove and a favourite pastime outside school was 'joyriding.' The freedom and the speed was a contrast to their lives. Whilst I was at the school one of the children was killed and later, in a separate accident, another was seriously injured loosing his arm, whilst another lost his brother to this pursuit. A taxi driver was also killed a father of three children. It was amazing that more weren't lost than that.

A very high status activity in eyes of the children was setting a police car on fire: they could really command a lot of respect in the eyes of their peers if they could claim responsibility for that. The damage that some of these children did in the area was phenomenal. These were the children who were right at the bottom of the pile in society. I was told that the vast majority would never get a job. Many would end up in prison. In many ways the school was their only hope in terms of escaping the lives they had and securing an improved future but they had no concept of the value of education. They could not even behave in an appropriate manner to participate in it properly. Before school, and teachers, can do their job home and parents must first do theirs. Little wonder most of them did not gain much benefit from the education system.

A sad consequence of this was a high turnover of staff. During my first term at the school, the pupils would repeatedly say to me: "When are YOU leaving?" as a greeting. They knew that teachers left because their behaviour was so bad. In a way the children were testing you, they desperately wanted you to care enough to stay and when people left it reinforced their belief that they weren't worth staying for. When I arrived there was a shortfall of teachers and the school was unable to provide all the required Maths, RE and PE lessons. I could hardly blame the staff for leaving but I was determined to stick it out. I decided that I would stay for at least five years in order to see some of the pupils pass all the way through the school. So when one of the pupils asked about leaving, I would now say: "I'm not going anywhere until you've done your exams and left school." I thought I owed it to them to make a commitment because most of them had suffered such a lot of instability in their lives.

The language the pupils used was terrible but after a while it became part of the normal routine and I ceased to be shocked by it. It was how they spoke, how they gained their 'street cred' with other pupils, and how they expressed their anger and frustration, but it set them apart from society. It was difficult to take them anywhere when they would show you up by their language. One of the pupils sitting an English exam once wrote: "When Romeo found out that Juliet was dead, he was fucking gutted." We constantly told them about their language but it was very difficult to change such long-term habits, like their smoking. Some of the children had smoked since they were five and were allowed to smoke at home. After a while, like other staff, I found I swore more myself.

Because of the hardship they had suffered some of the children seemed older than their years. You could hold an adult conversation with them and their sense of humour was subtle and sophisticated. Their behaviour and language were often inappropriate which meant they were sometimes very funny, sometimes without even meaning to be so. I enjoyed having small classes. It gave me the opportunity to get to know the pupils and work out the best ways to deal with them. Sometimes even getting the pupils into the classroom was an achievement. In order to keep them there, you had to be creative.

I was given responsibility for careers. Although many of the pupils had caring parents, they were not positive role models when it came to employment. I tried to make lessons as interactive as possible to encourage the pupils to participate in their lessons. For example, staging a mock interview where I would dress up as two prospective employees and the pupils would have to interview me for a job. In the first instance I would wear some horrible false teeth and red lipstick, dress unsuitably and act like a terrible interviewee. The pupils would have a list of questions that they had devised and would ask things like: "The job starts at 9 a.m., can you make it in for that time?" I would give them silly answers like: "I don't usually get up until half past nine, can I start at 10 a.m. instead?" Then I would go out of the class and come back in dressed more formally. I would be a model interviewee this time and they would have to choose which candidate to employ. Then I would come back in as the first interviewee and they would have to break the news to me that I hadn't got the job. At this point I once stayed in character and took offence, shouting at them and demanding why I didn't get the job. They loved doing this exercise, seeming to lose themselves in their role, and being surprisingly responsible in their own animated, expressive style. They would stay interested throughout the session because it was light-hearted.

If they did well I would often ring and tell their mums how good they had been. A lot of the parents had never received a good report about their child. The children loved this and would often ask me to do it, even accompanying me whilst I did. This was one of the most rewarding parts of my job. I also arranged work placements for the pupils. It was sometimes difficult to find the right placements for the pupils but I enjoyed trying to match them up with somewhere suitable. I thought it was the only chance some of them would get to have a taste of the working environment. It was also a way to integrate them into society because I often felt they were isolated, pushed out of the community because of their behaviour. Some of the pupils did really well in their placements which gave me a real sense of achievement. Although I would sometimes get called to go and collect them because they were misbehaving, such as chucking mortar about instead of using it to lay bricks.

Coming up to Christmas we would have a staff curry night; I made a curry and staff bought tickets. We would get all the children a selection box with the proceeds and arrange for Father Christmas to come to give them to the children. One of my ex-students from College, Tony, did Father Christmas and he came in for me as a favour. I would dress up as his fairy with a big silver star on a brush handle. Some people thought our children were too old at 11–16 and would not appreciate it, but they loved it. They would queue up and wait their turn, having missed things like this when they were little. He got a lot of orders for motorbikes! One afternoon as I walked down the corridor in my most ridiculous fairy outfit, a lilac tutu and a cerise pink satin top, an advisor from the authority was just arriving and going in the office with the head teacher. "That's Mrs Walker our head of year ten," I heard him say, very matter of factly as she looked at me very strangely.

Just as we finished for the Christmas holidays in 2002, my mum fell ill and had to go into hospital. She had been diagnosed with myloma, blood cancer, and Parkinson's disease previously but her mobility had deteriorated suddenly and she had become very confused. The admission was only supposed to be for a few days so that she could undergo tests and an assessment by a psychiatrist. However because it was Christmas many staff were off and her assessment with the psychiatrist didn't happen. Meanwhile she deteriorated further very rapidly and was placed on a high dependency ward. On 8th January, 2003, she passed away. It was a huge shock to me and the family. Even though we knew she was ill, the rate of her deterioration was disturbing and I struggled to cope with the loss. I was also now trying to support my father, who was devastated by what had happened.

Back at school, the circumstances were difficult for everyone. We rattled around in an unsuitable building, an old high school built for 600 pupils. There were just too many places for the children to hide, they even used to climb up above suspended ceilings and hide in there. One day a few of them hid under the stage, they set the stored Christmas tree and decorations on fire by smoking. The fire brigade had to turn out. It was a very serious incident and could have had tragic consequences. It put us in hot water with the local education authority that was in the process of building us a £4million new school. I became ensconced in a world where extreme behaviour was the norm and ceased to be shocked by it.

School was always under-staffed, even if we were officially fully staffed, because at least one or two teachers were always off sick. In March 2004 the head teacher went off due to anxiety. This caused even more disruption, although the deputy became Acting Head and did her best for the school. Although I tried to get on with all the pupils, some were a lot easier to relate to than others. Some of them appreciated what we were trying to achieve and through the bravado, you could see that they wanted to succeed and gain approval. Others were just nasty. One day while I was looking after the dinner queue, one pupil put his finger and thumb onto my throat. He came close to my face and said: "You want stabbing, you do." I had been trying to keep order in the line. I think he had a grudge against me because he wanted a work placement and I was struggling to find him one basically because he was a criminal. The police were called to the school and I gave a statement. He was not punished for this but it was taken into account when he later committed a further offence, he was then taken into custody. It was very difficult to keep motivated to help pupils such as this that was even at this age fully fledged criminals and bullies. It is also unfortunate that society's most vulnerable children are grouped with such individuals which actually compounds their deprivation.

We moved into the new school building after the Easter holidays in April 2004. There was a lot of organisational work to do and I put in a lot of additional work on Saturdays on a voluntary basis. Shortly after the move, our Special Educational Needs Co-ordinator, a senior member of staff, was suspended after child pornography was discovered on his computer and he was arrested. This was a huge blow particularly to staff who had trusted him. I had thought him to be a genuine and caring person and was annoyed at how gullible I had been. He had been second in management seniority to the deputy, meaning we were now also short of someone in that capacity. The school was in special measures having failed successive OFSTED inspections, the pupils were out of control and it felt like a pressure cooker ready to blow.

After the Whit Holiday in 2004 I found that I was struggling to cope. I did not feel well, I felt like an emotional wreck which I put down to my age. I made an appointment to see my doctor and asked him to put me on Hormone Replacement Therapy but he refused, saying I was too young and may need it more a couple of years down the line. I underwent tests for a possible hormone imbalance but these had proved negative. School was a very stressful place to work and I think I was still grieving for my mum, but what was driving me to despair was the fear that in some way the attacks on our home were related to my boys and I feared for their safety.

6   Teacher on Gun Charge

Ten days after the incident John and I were to attend the police station to find out if we were being charged. As we approached we were met by a bonny man with longish dark hair in a navy suit who asked if we were Walker and Cavanagh. He had been appointed as our solicitor. He told us that we were definitely being charged. "This could go on for up to a year. It could ruin your lives," he said. He also asked if we owned a house. When we said we did he shook his head. From which we presumed we may lose our house to pay for legal costs. It all sounded very ominous. We were then called into a room by a police officer and photographed holding a number, from a front and side view. We had our fingerprints taken and were DNA tested. The investigating DS carried out my test. He seemed particularly cheerful this morning.

There were a lot of forms to fill in, one of which was a charge sheet. In between all this I began to tell my solicitor about the campaign of harassment against us. "They are the police's star witnesses now," he said to my surprise. When I started to protest to the detective, the solicitor said: "Leave it Linda, save it for court," in a streetwise and supportive kind of way.

After some time we were taken into a small room and asked

for our employers' details. They were going to inform them of what we had been charged with! I was being charged with 16a firearms possession with intent to cause fear of unlawful violence, and affray. John was being charged with affray, from which we assumed they believed John when he denied having a gun. The solicitor said he would write to our employers but I knew things were hopeless for me. I would definitely be suspended. Despite the comments from the solicitor though, the full implications of our predicament had not yet sunk in.

Two days later as we walked towards the modern red brick building of Trafford Magistrate's Court, I felt a sense of apprehension. I could tell that John felt the same way. We eventually found our solicitor inside the court. He was a mature gentleman, quietly spoken with a genuine manner. He called us into a side room and told us that the magistrates would be referring the case to the Crown Court. This was because dealing with a firearms charge was outside their jurisdiction. We had not realised this and did not relish the thought of going to Crown Court.

In court, proceedings started very formally, we had to stand as the magistrates came in. They were two middle aged women and one man who were fairly formally dressed as were John and I. They peered at us over their glasses. I thought, "They don't know what to make of us, here on these serious charges." There were also two men taking notes; I later realised they must have been reporters when an article appeared in our local paper under the headline, *Teacher on gun charge.* A tall blonde young woman, who was the solicitor for the police, addressed the bench and outlined the charges. She read aloud the contents of my 999 call, including the swearing. The magistrates really peered over their glasses at us then. John is so inoffensive I had joked with him that the only way he could cause an affray was if the sun bounced off his bald head and he dazzled someone! The case was automatically referred to the Crown Court in Manchester for 23rd September, Donna's 20th birthday. What a birthday present! Her mother to be appearing at Crown Court.

The next day I was called into school for a meeting. I was to be suspended. I was told to take someone along with me, but this could not be my spouse. I stopped off on the way to ask my friend Sue, who worked at a private nursery around the corner from my school. We went to the school, which was still shut to the children for the school summer holiday. The acting head went through the terms of my suspension in accordance with the school's disciplinary procedure. I had never had anything to do with this procedure before. She said I was suspended from duty with immediate effect whilst investigations took place into an incident of a criminal nature. I could not visit the school or contact colleagues, although this was to prove difficult as I worked with my daughter Donna. My keys and the school mini bus had to be returned. The head was close to tears and I knew that she did not want to do this, she simply had no choice. She confirmed that I would be suspended on full pay. In truth, in the short-term, I welcomed this. I felt as though I needed a break after all the stress I had been under. I tried to make a joke of it to make her feel better. "I could do with a rise because I'll have more time to spend it," I said. She gasped and said: "Will you behave!" She was overcome by the seriousness of the situation whilst the full impact of the situation had still yet to dawn on me.

Sue went back to work, where an inquisitive colleague wanted to know why she had needed to leave in such a hurry.

"My friend has just ruined her life," said Sue.

"Why, has she had an affair?" asked the colleague.

"No, been there, done that and bought the t-shirt. It's much worse than that," Sue was very worried and concerned.

I felt aggrieved that we had been charged whilst what the youths had done had not been investigated. I decided to put an incident log together to provide documentary and photographic evidence of the damage done to our home. This, I thought, would prove what I had been telling the police when I was arrested, was true. I made an appointment to see my MP, Bev Hughes. I followed this up with a letter outlining my frustration at the police's failure to investigate the youths who had been harassing us. In the letter, I outlined my frustrations at the lack of response from the police in regard to our problems, that they seemed to tackle the symptoms of crime rather than the root causes. I wrote:

"In short they do what is expedient to obtain short-term goals rather than long-term aims. If this situation is allowed to continue, our system of law and order is doomed to fail. Someone in authority needs to know what is going on and how, how that they choose to police is potentially disastrous for the future of law and order in this country.

"What I mean is this, if a local beat bobby had picked up on the problem with local youths, he may have had cause to take one of them home, if he took him home he may have had cause to talk to his parents, if he had spoken to the parents, he may have raised – why is he out so late, wandering the streets and possibly getting into trouble? The parents may have acknowledged this concern and taken some action to supervise their child better. This may have helped to solve our problem.

"Our problem is now society's problem, the case is going to cost a lot of professional time and that is big money – probably ours, they may take our home. I may lose my job and John his. I am a professional teacher, I took years to train and cost thousands of pounds, as did John. We are/were a valuable commodity to society."

In return, I received an extremely encouraging letter informing me that she had written to the police, asking them to outline what action they had taken to establish if the youths had been responsible for the vandalism and harassment. She also wanted a record from me showing when incidents had taken place and what action if any the police had taken. I found her to be very open and helpful this was the beginning of a very long and fruitful correspondence with her.

7   Disillusionment Setting In

On Thursday, 23rd September we had our appointment at Crown Court. It was the beginning of a saga that was taking over our lives and seemed to be replacing my full-time job in terms of the time it consumed. We were worried about being late and had arrived so early that the court was not even open yet so we went for breakfast in a café around the corner under The Portland Hotel. The solicitor had advised us that the evidence the police had was incriminating, particularly the 999 call. Also if we were to plead guilty, we would get a lighter sentence because we would get credit for saving the time and trouble of a trial. I did not feel that what I had done was sufficient to warrant such serious charges. It had never been my intention to harm anyone. He had further advised John that perhaps it was safer for him to also plead guilty to avoid a possible prison sentence of up to three years!

After being security checked, we walked around the court looking for our solicitor. We found our names on one of the lists and sat outside the allocated court. At about 10.25 a.m. we were called in but our solicitor had still not arrived. We told the usher and he said that we were entitled to legal representation, so we did not go in. We didn't know what to do for the best.

While not wanting to go in without a solicitor, we also did not want to appear militant and antagonise the judge. Eventually, after calling for a representative of the company to attend on the public address system, a stout busy woman turned up in a gown and wig. She was from the company representing us but was on another case and said she would stand in for us. We had to stand in the dock again, standing up when the judge entered. He looked like he was straight out of a Robin Hood film in his outfit, like the Sheriff of Nottingham and that is how unreal it felt to me.

Before he came in John had said to me, in his usual reassuring way: "It was not long ago that a judge had the power to take your life and put you to death." I replied: "Yes, but you had to murder someone first," with a smile. The judge asked our representative something about the case but she had to declare she knew nothing. He set a date for Friday, 26th November, for the 'plea and directions' hearing. That would be, we assumed, when someone would eventually ask us how we were going to plead.

The following day John had an idea. He suggested I should make a complaint to the Independent Police Complaints Commission (IPCC) so I decided to write them a letter. I started the letter:

"I write to you on behalf of myself and my family who are citizens of impeccable character. We unfortunately have been victims of local yobs who have led a campaign of harassment and vandalism against us for over two years." And I ended the letter:

"I am not proud of what I did, I am not saying it was right or that I deserve a medal, I know I did wrong and I am deeply sorry. I am a person who has been driven to the brink of her sanity. If I have done wrong then I deserve to be investigated, I am not above the law, but by the same rule my complaint about what those youths did on the night of Friday 13th/14th August should be investigated. They are not above the law."

Regarding the investigating officer I wrote:

"He chooses to forget their questionable character and work with them when it suits him. I am not a criminal."

I enclosed a copy of the letter from my MP Bev Hughes, who had also written to Greater Manchester Police (GMP) following our meeting. She wrote: *"Since April this year, Mrs Walker has experienced more than four separate incidents including burglary, vandalism to the house and cars, harassment and abusive phone calls. All these incidents were reported to the police, who attended only in relation to one report, on 11th August regarding abusive phone calls. I would be grateful if you could let me know what action has been taken regarding these incidents. In relation to the incidents of the 13th/14th August which led to the current charges against Mrs Walker, I am unclear as to what investigation and identification is ongoing of the youths who harassed Mrs Walker on that evening, and would be grateful if you could let me have details of what action is being taken. Obviously, I am not in a position to have a full account of what happened that evening and clearly one cannot condone individual citizens taking the law into their own hands, although I am not suggesting that this is what Mrs Walker attempted to do. Nonetheless, she makes an important point when she says that it is at least in part due to the failure of the police to take these anti-social behaviour incidents seriously that led to the levels of frustration that evident on the night of 13th/14th August."*

On 1st October, the police sent a letter of reply to Bev Hughes in which they referred to the youths involved as 'innocent.' In her reply she astutely wrote:

"*In relation to the incident on 10.04.04 (Burglary) and 01.08.04 (Damage to motor vehicle), you say it is policy for police not to attend if there is no evidence. It is not clear to me how the police know there is no evidence if they don't attend to try to collect any evidence.*

"*In relation to the incident on 14.08.04, you refer to the youths involved as 'innocent'. I asked in my earlier letter what investigations had been conducted in relation to the youths involved and Mrs Walker's claims that some of the youths that night had been perpetrating a series of incidents over the summer and one well known to her family. I would be grateful to know what investigations have been undertaken of the young people in relation to the incident on 14th August and those earlier in the summer.*"

She pertinently closed the letter by stating:

"*It is also important that the full picture – not a one-sided picture – is elucidated in this case and it seems so far that little has been done to establish what responsibility the youths concerned may have had for persistent harassment and intimidation of the family.*"

Following our disappointment with our solicitor we had changed firms and at a meeting with our new solicitor we were, by now, well aware of the serious nature of the charges brought against us and so were more prepared for what she said. She told us that if we didn't want to plead guilty, no one was going to attempt to force us. However, we needed to be aware of the risks associated with this. The factors in our favour were that a relevant defence in law did exist and we may well get the sympathy of the jury. The factors against us were the 999 call and the fact that the type of weapon had no relevance whatsoever. I could still have been charged with the same offence had I been holding a banana under a newspaper, an air pistol, or a real firearm. She said she had listened to our taped police interviews and felt uneasy about them.

A further appointment was arranged, where we met Sue Ann, a trainee solicitor who was to deal with our case from now on under the guidance of the solicitor. Sue Ann was lovely, a very pretty girl with a look of Kate Moss about her. Although she was quite young and nervous, we soon discovered that she was very meticulous and conscientious in her work. She would never forget a single detail about our case. We were to get to know Sue Ann quite well over the next few months.

On the morning of Friday, 24th November, 2004, we attended our last hearing before the trial – the committal hearing. As we walked to the court from the car park, we noticed a photographer with an expensive-looking long lens camera. As we walked past him, he kept clicking photographs of us.

"There must be someone famous here today. Why is he taking pictures of us?" I said to John. I thought he must have mistaken us for someone else. When we went into the court building we saw the man in the 'lady in the lake' case and presumed the photographer must have been there for something to do with him.

Sue Ann was at court to guide and support us, unlike the last time we had appeared. We were supposed to be meeting our barristers but Sue Ann said that unfortunately, mine was tied up with another case in Sheffield. Instead John's barrister, a lady called Mary, would represent me as well. We had a meeting with Mary but she knew nothing of my case. She had not had the opportunity to do any preparation for my case at all. Later, I wondered whether if she had known more, the case might never have gone to trial on the serious charges which it did. It would have been within her rights to object to the charges and argue that they were inappropriately extreme.

The barrister told John that she did not think he had a lot to worry about and that he was probably charged to put pressure on me. We didn't understand this but she went on to explain that they may offer us a plea bargain. If I was to plead guilty, they would probably offer to drop the charge against John. John was incensed. I said that John would rather go to prison than let them use him against me. He later said: "Thank you for volunteering me for that Linda." But I knew he was only joking. John thought it was immoral to charge someone for an offence and use one person against another in this way.

Turning to me, the barrister said: "Your case is a lot more serious. Our main concern is to keep you out of prison." She seemed to think it highly likely that I would go to prison, based on the seriousness of the charges. I told her that I was not prepared to plead guilty to charges which I didn't consider I had committed. "OK, as long as you are aware of the risks and implications," she said. Although I was quite shocked about how seriously she took the possibility of my imprisonment, I thought: "She doesn't know anything about my case." I had not been the aggressor when I fired the air pistol he had approached me, I was the one who felt under threat.

As we went into court, I was hoping it would be as long as possible until the trial began. This was partly because I was worried about the case but to be perfectly honest it was also because I was enjoying being off work for the first time in my 26 year career. It was only since finishing work that I had fully realised how much pressure I had put myself under as a working mum. People think teaching is short hours and long holidays but anyone who is, or has been a teacher, will know that is not the case. The job carries on when the children are not there. Now that I was getting a bit of distance from the job for the first time, I could see how much pressure I had been under. I almost felt that I would rather go to prison than return to my job. But at that time I did not realised why I felt this way.

The Judge asked us to stand while he outlined the charges against us: firearms and affray for me and affray for John. He asked us individually how we pleaded. We answered: "Not guilty" and were allowed to sit down. He addressed our barrister about the case, but she could not answer his questions. He was very sharp with her because she was clearly not prepared.

"Have you got a defence prepared for these defendants? You are supposed to be ready for trial," he said. She tried to explain that she only represented John but he was clearly not interested in her excuses. He consulted a diary and said: "January". The barrister asked for a later hearing, citing that the Christmas period would give them less time to prepare, but he was very abrupt and gave her the week beginning the 31st of January. I thought: "I hope **he** isn't our judge for the trial."

Sue Ann had a big job ahead of her for the rest of November, reviewing the case against us and preparing our defence statements and those of our witnesses, Donna, Rob and my son Craig, who had all seen some of what happened that night and could talk about the background to the incident. I paid several visits to my barrister's chambers in Manchester in the period running up to Christmas. The case against us comprised of: the 999 call, our police interviews, the police case summary, witness statements from Police Witness 1 (PW 1), the youth I had had the altercation with and Police Witness 2 (PW 2), the one who had stepped out from behind the wall and the arresting officers. The police case summary began:

"Shortly after 00.15 hrs on Saturday 14th August 2004, the defendants Linda Walker and John Cavanagh were in the lounge of their home address, ——— ——— ——— (address),

Flixton, when it was discovered that someone had placed a plastic washing up bottle on the roof of a car parked upon the driveway at the front of her home. Neither defendant nor any other person saw the person place this bottle upon the car, and the defendants will state the bottle belonged to them and had been left in the rear garden. Linda Walker then assumed that persons had been prowling about the property and she rushed outside to find the prowlers whilst the defendant John Cavanagh went upstairs to fix the fuse in the security light which covers the front of the house."

That persons had been prowling on our property was not an 'assumption.' Unless he was suggesting that the gallon container full of liquid had levitated from the back garden to on top of the car at the front. It went on:

"Linda Walker will state that she saw a group of youths some distance away from her house (200 yards) on Flixton Road, and saw one of the youths place a road sign in the road into a position where it would be struck by passing vehicles so she went to confront the youths.

"The witness —— (PW 1) will state that he was walking on Flixton Road with friends including —— (PW 2) when he heard a woman scream: "Psychos". He turned to see the defendant Linda Walker rushing up the road towards him. (He knows her as Linda as he went to school with her son.)

"Linda Walker then accused —— (PW 1) of placing items into the roadway and continued to call him a "Psycho". She was red in the face with rage and would not be placated."

After I returned with the guns, the statement claims that John also arrived and threatened PW 1 prior to me discharging the air pistol. John did not arrive until after this.

"—— (PW 1) by this time was frightened and at this point some of his friends including —— (PW 2) had walked to the corner of Delamere Rd/Flixton Rd. Linda Walker then raised her right arm pointing the handgun towards —— (PW 1) feet then fired the weapon 4 or 5 times.

"He will state that by this time he was terrified."

A summary of the incident was included in the paperwork provided for court by the Criminal Prosecution Service (CPS) which read:

BRIEF OUTLINE OF ALLEGATIONS AND ISSUES

The defendant Linda Walker approached local youths in the street after midnight with a shotgun and a handgun screaming at them. She discharged the gun and shot 5–6 bullets at the feet of the youths.

LIKELY ISSUES:

Admissions made in interview by both defendants

That the incident had been exaggerated to this extent was a shock to us. It made me sound like Clint Eastwood in a wild west film!

8 Conflicting Accounts

The Police Witnesses' responses although not wholly accurate and conflicting with each other were also revealing. The Statement of PW 1 began:

"At 1830 hrs on Friday 13th August I left home to meet my friends for a night out in Sale.

"During the course of the evening I had drank four cans of lager."

He said that they had caught a bus back to Urmston at about 11.15 p.m., back to Woodsend Road. One of his friends then left to go home whilst he and a remaining friend went to a takeaway on Woodsend Road, where they saw some friends and chatted for about 10 minutes. After that, they left and walked towards the "general direction of Flixton Road".

At this point on his journey he would have passed our cul-de-sac, our home stands back 35 yards from Flixton Road, about 200 yards from Dillons' newsagents.

"As we approached Dillons' newsagents we met PW 2 and his friend whom I only know him as —— (nickname). All four of us continued to walk up Flixton Road prior to the junction of Delamere Road. I then heard a woman screaming 'Psychos' behind us. She was some 50 yards away from us."

He said: "—— (his associate) made off down Delamere Road. I remained there because I hadn't done anything.

"I kept on telling her to calm down, she was furious and her face was red with rage. I tried to reason with her but she just would not listen. She then said she had guns at home."

He said that about five or ten minutes later, he saw me walking back towards them with the guns.

"I could see she had a rifle under her left arm. The rifle was wooden with a metal barrel but the barrel was open into a 90 degree angle from the stock. I then saw a black metal hand gun in her right hand. Her arm was straight down by her side and the gun was pointing to the floor."

He went on to say: "I kept on telling her it wasn't me and to calm down. She then said to me: "Look I've got guns here! This is what you'll get if you come to my house again!"

He continued: "The woman still six foot in front of me was still shouting. Then, she raised her right arm about a 45 degree angle, with the black hand gun in her right hand and pointed it slightly to the left of my feet. She then shot five or six times from the hand gun. The shots were about five foot from my feet. I was terrified. I thought she was about to shoot me. I screamed at her to stop. She was going to hurt someone or me. She then said she had rung the police. She said I was in trouble. I disagreed and said that she was. I told her that I was going to wait for the police too. When this was still happening the male was stood outside the youth club some 10 yards away. Then a dark coloured Astra pulled up near to us and two men in shirts got out and approach us. I was relieved to see someone had come to my assistance!"

The second police witness said that at around 12.30 a.m. he was with a friend sitting on a bench in Flixton Road, opposite the junction with Delamere Road.

"I heard some shouting coming from the direction of the bus stop situated on the other side of Flixton Road about 100 yards further down towards Flixton. I then saw another friend, —— (PW 1's associate), who was walking along Flixton Road from the bus stop towards —— (nickname) and myself. Another friend, —— (PW 1's first name) was walking up behind —— (the associate) and he was about 20 yards behind him.

"I could see that —— (PW 1) was stood about 10 yards from a woman and that they were both arguing with each other. I could not tell what was being said but I could just hear raised voices."

He continued: "Both —— (PW 1) and the woman continued to walk along Flixton Road towards us. —— (PW 1's assoc) reached the bench first and he said: "there is a psycho woman chasing us." —— (PW 1's assoc) then ran into Flixton Fields which is situated behind the bench we were sat on."

Then, his account differs from that of PW 1, who portrayed himself as an innocent victim who tried to calm me down using reason. He recollects him goading me to go and get my guns.

"—— (PW 1) and the woman arrived at the bench and they were still arguing whilst they were both stood directly in front of me and about two yards apart. I heard the woman say: "Don't make me go and get my shotgun." PW 1 replied: "Go and get your shotgun then."

"Then the woman said: "It's not a shotgun, it's an air rifle." —— (PW 1) replied: "Go and get it then." The woman then walked off towards the bus stop on Flixton Road and out of sight."

When I a short time later returned with the guns, he said:

"At this time I was stood about 10 yards away from her,

on the opposite site of Delamere Road. I could see that she was carrying an air rifle which was tucked under her right arm. It had a brown wooden handle and a metal barrel. She was also carrying a small dark coloured pistol in her left hand.

"The woman and —— (PW 1) walked over to each other. They were stood face to face with only inches between them. The woman told —— (PW 1) to move his feet which he refused to do. The woman then discharged the pistol towards ——'s (PW 1's) left foot. She again told him to move his feet and each time he refused, she fired the pistol towards his feet. I do not think any of the pellets hit —— (PW 1). She fired the pistol about five or six times.

"She also told (PW 1) to lie down in the middle of the road which he refused to do." This was not alleged by PW 1 himself. PW 2 also claimed that John appeared with a small silver hand pistol. His statement ended: "I personally did not feel in fear of my personal safety but I did fear for the personal safety of my friend —— (PW 1)."

His version portrayed him as an onlooker, and omits that he had also 'fronted up' to me along with PW 1, whilst the other youths had chanted our names.

The reports from the arresting plain clothes officers were straightforward accounts of how they had spotted me with the guns whilst they happened to be driving past.

Our defence documents were to include the previous convictions of the police witnesses. These we believed were an important part of our case. They would prove that the 'witnesses' who were being put forward as 'victims' by the police, were of dubious character. Further, they would add weight to my claim that one of them was capable of targeting our house and putting a road sign in the middle of the road.

PW 1 had a string of convictions, including several for offences the same as those perpetrated against my family, PW 2 also had several police cautions and convictions on record.

9   Mitigation and Uncertainty

My defence team asked me to gather several character references from friends and colleagues who knew me in different capacities. Nigel Haslam, the head teacher who had appointed me to my job at School wrote a very complimentary reference for me. He stated, *"She always undertook her responsibilities in an extremely professional manner, dedicating many additional hours in order to fully meet the needs of the young people. She exhibited an empathetic approach to working with these extremely disturbed young people. There are a significant number of them who were extremely grateful and appreciative of her efforts, who successfully held down their placements and succeeded in transferring to college or the world of work. Her efforts were praised by both OFSTED and HMI Inspectors when they visited the school and they commented that her areas of work were a strength of the school."*

Christine Conway, who was my Educational Support Worker at school prior to Donna, wrote: *"Linda has a brilliant relationship with children at school. She is calm yet firm and handles confrontational situations with sensitivity and professionalism. Her natural warmth and sense of humour make children feel secure in her presence. In the two years I have worked with her I have never seen her lose her temper with a child. A lot of children at school have a problem with attending for one reason or another and many of our children have missed long periods of school. Children often come to school because of Linda's efforts and because they see her as a friend. She always treats them respectfully and gives them many chances to succeed even though they may not always take them. The fact she is no longer at school is a sad loss for all, children and staff alike, and school life has become less fun because of it."*

Susan Curtis, one of my closest friends, wrote: *"I have known Linda for 20 years since she worked as a colleague with my mother. Fifteen years ago I moved into the road next to Linda and after the death of my husband Linda became a friend in a million to me. She was a great support helping me with my children when I was on my own. Linda loves organising people and making sure everyone is happy. Linda is a lovely mum working hard to support and keep her children happy and healthy. With the love and care that she has given to them she now has a very close family life living with her partner John. She will always go that extra mile to help people and so many people have gained from knowing her."*

Another of my closest friends, Barbara Crawford, wrote: *"I have known Linda for 36 years since we were at secondary school together."* She commented that I am a loyal and trustworthy friend and an excellent mother to my children.

I felt quite humbled by these references. I thought that they were being extra nice about me because they were so upset about what was happening to us. They were as upset as we were. They knew I was not a violent person.

After Christmas my solicitor commissioned a psychiatric report. The doctor was provided with background documents about the case. I went along to her office in Old Trafford for the interview. She was a little older than me and empathised with me regarding my concerns about the menopause affecting my emotional stability. The interview took two hours and the resulting report was to form part of my defence.

She detailed the stresses I had been under at work and we had been under at home, and how we had contacted the police and Victim Support. Her brief was to comment on my mental state and the stresses and other facts affecting this.

She wrote: "When I saw Mrs Walker she was entirely cooperative with the interview. She made good eye contact, and it was possible to form a good rapport with her. Her speech was normal in rate, form and content. At times during the interview she appeared quite distressed, particularly when talking about her fears that it was her sons who were being targeted by the vandalism. However for most of the interview she was able to remain quite calm. Her mood appeared within normal limits, with no abnormal elation or depression. She did not express suicidal ideas. There was no evidence of psychosis, or of cognitive impairment."

The psychiatrist gave a diagnosis at the end of her report, based on her analysis of my mental state at the time of the incident.

She wrote: "I would diagnose Mrs Walker as suffering from an adjustment disorder. The International Classification of Diseases, version 10, (ICD–10) describes this as "states of subjective distress and emotional disturbance, usually interfering with social functioning and performance, and arising in the period of adaptation to a significant life change or to the consequences of a stressful life event".

She added: "I am of the opinion that as a result of the various stressful life events that Ms Walker had suffered in recent years she had developed an adjustment disorder manifesting as irritability and changeable mood. I would regard her being in the early stages of the menopause as one of the stresses to which she has been subjected, rather than as the primary cause of her problems. The presence of an adjustment disorder would make Ms Walker more likely to overreact to further stresses, even minor ones." It then went on to state, "This would not make her unaware of the consequences of her actions, nor would it render her incapable of forming intent." Which confirmed that I am sane.

My defence team had also acquired a letter from Victim Support confirming that I had been in touch with them about the harassment at our home. The Deputy Manager of Victim Support in Sale, wrote: "We have been in contact with Linda following very traumatic incidents, which have occurred at the above address. These have left Linda and her family feeling unsafe and fearful at home. Linda has expressed her frustration and feelings of helplessness with being a victim of crime several times; unfortunately as a result she retaliated and has said how sorry she is now for her actions. We would be very grateful if you could take all the circumstances into account."

I also supplied a record of my appointment with the gynaecology clinic at Trafford General Hospital, which I had attended in September 2004. The psychiatric report confirmed I was suffering from an 'adjustment disorder' caused by the stress I was under. The menopause was only a part of this. However, the notice of the appointment proved that I had been having problems and had taken steps I thought appropriate to address these. In our discussion about this, the psychiatrist had told me that extreme stress can produce the same symptoms as menopause. I also later found out that the 'out of body experience' I had felt on the night was also a symptom of extreme stress.

The defence submitted two official definitions of what constitutes an 'Affray'. Our barristers planned to argue that there were no grounds for the charge of 'Affray' against John because there was no evidence to suggest that he had threatened anyone. In my case, they would argue that 'Affray' was not appropriate either because I had not attempted violence against anyone. I had deliberately pointed the gun at the pavement. The first definition stated that: "the threat of violence cannot be made by the use of words alone – either orally or in writing. There must be some act or gesture amounting to a threat of unlawful violence. The prosecution must show – as with violent disorder – that the assailant intended to use or threaten violence or were aware that their conduct might amount to violence or the threat of violence."

The second definition, taken from CPS Legal Guidance, repeated the point that words were not adequate to amount to Affray in law.

"The seriousness of the offence lies in the effect that the behaviour of the accused has on members of the public who may have been put in fear. There must be some conduct, beyond the use of words, which is threatening and directed towards a person or persons. Mere words are not enough."

I dispute that the 'victim' in this case was put in fear. He had encouraged me to get the guns and to fire them. Further, the definition states that 'Affray should be considered in circumstances of serious and indiscriminate violence." This incident was by no means indiscriminate. The charge in our opinion was wholly inappropriate for either of us. Examples of the type of conduct appropriate to a charge of 'Affray' are listed in the CPS legal guidance, they included the indiscriminate throwing of objects directed towards a group of people in circumstances where serious injury was, or was likely, to be caused, such as throwing bricks into a crowd. Another example quoted was, "The wielding of a weapon of a type or in a manner likely to cause people substantial fear for their safety or *a person armed with a weapon who, when approached by police officers, brandishes the weapon and threatens to use it against them.*" In contrast, I had not wielded the weapon in a frightening way and when the police asked me to put it down, I had done so immediately.

We had hoped that at the very least, the harassment would stop now that things had been brought to a head. In December 2004, however, as we prepared to go to trial, James' car was broken into and his stereo equipment stolen. Prior to James starting his job as a junior quantity surveyor, his car was a wreck and I thought that he might as well spend his spare time renovating it, so I offered to lend him the money to do it. He seemed to think 'doing it up' meant kitting it out with the latest stereo equipment and turning it into a mobile disco! On 22nd December 2004 the £600 worth of hi-fi equipment was stolen from his car. I phoned the police, who came to take fingerprints but they did not find any. The following day I took a Christmas card to the social club next to our road. In the office was a series of monitors linked to CCTV cameras. One covered the part of our road where James parked his car. I phoned the police and told them that the club kept the footage of the tapes for a month. They promised to attend. Just before the month was up, I phoned again. The police never attended to collect the footage from the CCTV camera so any possible evidence was lost.

That Christmas I tried to put it all out of my mind and enjoy myself with the family as usual. As I wrapped my presents, though, I couldn't help wondering where I would be in a year's time. I had already started decorating the house in case we had to sell it if I lost my job. I had also started to think of alternative career options and had been to look at a potential sandwich shop near to our house. I knew that if I lost the case, I would most likely lose my job and the career I had worked hard to achieve. I wondered if I would even have enough money to buy any presents next Christmas, if I would be in the same house, or if I would even be in prison. It felt as if my whole life was in other people's hands. After 25 years of having the security of my job, suddenly everything was uncertain.

PART 2

The Trial

11   Not Even a Shred of Evidence

The trial started on Tuesday, 1st February, 2005. It was long and complicated and spanned eight days. It was originally to be held at Minshull Street Crown Court, Manchester, but had been moved at the last minute to Stockport Magistrates' Court, which took overflow Crown Court cases from Manchester.

Our barrister's told us that a plea bargain was on the table. The prosecution was willing to drop John's charge of affray in exchange for my guilty plea to a lesser, but still serious, section 18 firearms offence. John's barrister, now a man, had told the prosecution that we were not interested, in no uncertain terms, before they even put it to us. He knew our minds and we were happy with his approach. We felt confident they would not be able to prove the charge against John and I didn't intend to plead guilty to any such charge. I was hopeful that the charges being so serious could in a way go in our favour because they seemed so extreme when compared with the evidence. I could go to prison for ten years and John for three!

The trial began with legal formalities and the swearing in of the jury. The same group had been on jury service the previous week and the judge said that the trial had to be finished by Friday in order to release them. The prosecution barrister, a tall slim man, wore a wide pinstripe suit under his gown and his hair looked too grey for his years. He began by making his opening speech telling the court that John and I were teachers who lived together.

I was shocked that after all our prolific complaining about the police not investigating the youths and even after the intervention of my MP in this matter, he used the fact that the police had not investigated against us. He stated regarding my allegations against the youths of their involvement in the crime and vandalism at our house and placing a road sign in the road,

"I tell you now there is not a shred of evidence in this case to support that contention." And, regarding my actions,

"She rushed up to him, stopped in front of him and accused him, the crown says quite falsely without any evidence at all, of having placed this plastic water bottle on top of her car and she called him to his face psycho."

He picked the pistol up using a pen through the handle, as if to imply that touching it would be too dangerous. He said "This is a Walther CP88 pellet firing gas powered pistol and it is a lethal weapon within the provisions of the Firearms Act."

The 999 call was played to the court. What I had said was very incriminating. I had stated I intended to go out and shoot people and this was taken literally by the barrister. As it was played, he punctuated it with comments such as:

"She was told, perhaps again unsurprisingly, by the police employee on the other end of the phone to calm down and that she should not be doing it, because she was admitting, effectively, an arrestable offence."

He seemed very pleased with the contents of the tape.

"The crown invites you to accept that really she could not care less what the officer was saying to her on the other end of the telephone; she had made up her mind as to what she was going to do with these weapons."

He then turned to the incident itself. According to PW 2, John was also armed with a small, silver, shiny pistol, which he held by his side. He claimed that John was with me when I had approached the youths prior to me discharging the air pistol, "John Cavanagh then arrived, he stood directly in front of —— (PW 1), effectively standing in his face and, in a rather formal, threatening and intimidating manner.

"Mrs Walker then raised her right arm and pointed the handgun to the left of ——'s (PW 1) feet and discharged it about five or six times into the tarmac. He was not struck by any of the pellets, but you can imagine the potential impact."

I felt like we were Bonny and Clyde sat there in the dock, while the jury looked at us.

The barrister now moved on to the arrival of the police.

"Mrs Walker was still in possession of her rifle and pistol at that time and the police officers, from some distance away, were telling her, as you see on television programmes, to put those weapons down and eventually she did so. She was arrested on the basis of being in possession of a firearm with intent to cause fear of violence. "I'm going to my MP" was her initial response. She went straight to Stretford police station instead, where she was later interviewed." He had strategically used the word 'eventually'. My enquiry about why are you arresting me and not him was not mentioned. My assertion to contact my MP made to sound absurd.

He summarised John's police interview, beginning by making an inference about the amount of alcohol we had consumed that night. He re-iterated, "There is no evidence at all to suggest that —— (PW 1) or —— (PW 2), or indeed anybody else in the group, had caused any difficulties at all at Mrs Walker's house."

To conclude his opening statement he continued:

"There is no dispute that Mrs Walker was in possession of both those weapons on the 14th August. What her intention was when she had them is a matter for you, the jury, to determine, having heard the evidence, but of course you are entitled to draw common sense conclusions (inferences) from the facts as you find them to be. Somebody in that sort of irate state, who arms themselves, checks the gun is loaded, discharges it in their own house and then goes outside and discharges it within feet of an individual that she does not know, what else could that person intend, in those circumstances, other than to make —— (PW1) in this case believe that he would be the victim of unlawful violence. And the Crown says this was all unlawful violence because self defence does not really get off the ground here; this woman was not in any form of fear or in threat; she could have stayed locked behind the front door and waited for the police."

The prosecution barrister was obviously impressive as the initial press coverage of that first day was very negative, especially the account provided by Eleanor Moritz on the local BBC television news. When we got home the phone kept ringing. An ex-colleague, who had been assistant principal at the college where I had previously worked and John still worked, rang to ask if he could help. He offered to be a character reference for us. He said he could not believe what he had seen on the television. This was when friends and family started to get worried, saying the TV reporting made me sound awful. They were unable to associate with the picture painted of us as hateful and malicious to young people. It was so unlike the Linda and John they knew who had worked all their lives to help young people – their own children as well as those of others. John's brother and his wife phoned to invite us round for tea.

While we were there, I told John that I thought it was about time he told his own children Rachel and Oliver, before they saw us on television. We decided to ring them when we got home. Rachel said that her fiancé had just seen us on the television but had not caught what it was about. When we told them what was happening, they were shocked. Oliver was not at home so we sent him a text asking if he was alright. He texted back: 'just going to pictures txt u later'. He had obviously not heard anything yet. We decided to ask him and his sister over for tea the next day to explain everything. For now, we had to concentrate on getting ready to appear in court the following day.

12   The Revelation

The next morning, we were back in court. Before the jury were brought back in, my barrister wanted to address the judge to ask his permission to confront the prosecution witnesses with their criminal records. Although it is not normal practice to reveal this information, my barrister argued that it was relevant in this case as PW 1's convictions were for offences I alleged he and his associates had committed against us. The judge, who seemed to operate on the principle of: "Why say a word when 5,000 will do?" deliberated on every conceivable angle before eventually allowing the request. I saw this as a good indication that the trial was going well for us.

PW 1 was called to give his evidence. Unsurprisingly he left out all the detail which incriminated him. He did not mention placing a road sign in the road then standing back to watch what happened. He claimed that he and three others including PW 2 were simply standing and chatting on the street when I approached them shouting and screaming. He also failed to admit fronting up to me in a threatening manner. His version was that he did nothing to stand up to me at all, that he tried to placate me and told me to calm down because he was concerned, for my welfare.

The barrister asked how he felt when I discharged the gun.

"I got scared at that point."

"Why?"

"Because she had pulled the trigger a few times in my direction and she was pretty angry, so I thought maybe, even if she didn't mean to shoot me, she could do it by accident."

"Did you say anything to her?"

"I told her to stop and calm down, someone could get hurt."

Then it was my barrister's turn to cross-examine the witness. She questioned him about his night out that evening up to the point where he and his friend were walking past our house. He denied that he had called at our house and when questioned if he had ever been to our house uninvited he replied no.

"The reason you remember, or you know, ——— ——— Drive is a cul-de-sac is because you have been there uninvited, have you not?"

"What, in the house?"

"Certainly in the garden?"

"When?"

"Have you been there in the garden at all?"

"Whose garden?"

"Linda Walker's house in ——— ——— Drive; have you been in her garden uninvited?"

"No."

"Any particular reason why you needed me to be specific about when, if you have never been there?"

"Not uninvited, no."

He claimed that he had been to our house once at the invitation of my son, but that was a long time ago.

My barrister held a list of the witness' criminal convictions in her hand. The following is taken from court transcripts.

"You have been involved in trouble before, have you not?"

"Yes."

"How old were you back in November, 2003?"

"On the 13th November you were 18?"

"Yes."

"Do you remember being in Trafford Juvenile Court on the 13th November, 2003?"

"Yes."

"Do you remember being sentenced for a number of matters of burglary and theft?"

"Yes."

"You burgled a non-dwelling?"

"Yes."

"You pleaded guilty to that?"

"Yes."

"You burgled with intent to cause unlawful damage in a non dwelling; you pleaded guilty to that?"

"Yes."

"You were found on enclosed premises for an unlawful purpose?"

"Yes."

"What was that, do you remember?"

"Yes."

"What was it?"

"We stole some boxes of chocolate from the school tuck shop."

"Was that at night?"

"Yes."

"Early hours of the morning?"

"Yes."

"What time?"

"Maybe 9/10 o'clock."

"Your own school?"

"I had left."

"You had left, but was it the school you used to go to?"

"Yes."

As he said this alarm bells started to ring in my head and I started to remember!

"Were you alone on that occasion?"

"No I was with —— —— (his associate) and —— —— (another local youth)."

One of these youths being the same one we alleged he was with when he came up our drive that night.

She continued: "What about the first burglary I read out to you, who were you with then?"

"It's the same thing really; we went in and out a few times."

"There are three altogether of being found on enclosed premises?"

"Yes."

"You say they all relate to the tuck shop do you?"

"Yes."

"What about the criminal damage matter?"

"We broke a door to get in."

"With —— —— (his associate) again?"

"Yes."

All of a sudden everything became clear. In the autumn of 2003 two Police Officers had come to our house to speak to James. They wanted to know if he knew anything about a break in at school into the tuck shop, which he did. He knew his ex-friend —— was involved along with this lad. This I think was part of the reason why he no longer bothered with him he said he wasn't the same anymore. Although he had knowledge of the incident he declined to give a statement as he did not want to attend court. I now realised that this was the incident for which PW 1 had been prosecuted. They must have thought my son was to blame for their convictions! It was strange because it wasn't so much the damage that occurred that was distressing, although that was bad enough, it was that things kept happening and we didn't know who it was, and we didn't know <u>why</u> it was happening to us. So despite the circumstances in which I found out, I felt relieved.

He was then cross-examined by John's lawyer. He could not say one thing that John had said or done to him that was offensive.

The witness was then re-examined by the prosecution's barrister.

"It has been suggested to you more than once that you, or you and your friend, went to this house that night, did something to the car, in terms of this washing up bottle, and it has been suggested too that you have been accused of making nuisance phone calls because you had a mobile phone. First and foremost, have the police at any stage ever spoken to you or arrested you or asked you to come to the police station to answer questions about any incident or vandalism or nuisance phone calls in relation to this family?"

"No."

More's the pity!

This confirmed that our requests for the Police to investigate the youths had been ignored, and now we knew why. After I had complained to the IPCC the complaint was accepted and passed to GMP for them to investigate. The non-investigation of the youths involved was a main item of the complaint at that stage. We had received a letter from GMP that stated, "because the events were subject to criminal proceedings; the matter would be held in abeyance until the outcome of those proceedings was known". This was very convenient for their case now because they could make sweeping statements such as this that seemed to vindicate their witnesses in the eyes of the jury.

"You say you were not involved in any of those incidents, is that right?"

"That's right."

"You have been through your previous convictions with the jury in some detail; always pleaded guilty, is that right?"

"Yes."

"Do you have any convictions for violence?"

"No."

This was technically true. A violent charge in relation to an incident on 2nd October, 2004, was only pending at that point.

The barrister stepped down.

The witness was free to leave.

Another aspect of our police complaints, John had also now complained, was that the charges brought were excessive. I had objected that by leaving matters in abeyance those excessive charges may have resulted in us receiving convictions or even custodial sentences. I thought this would give the complaint more priority, as a safeguard against injustice. But it would seem that this was not the case.

13   Witnesses Dragged Out of Bed

The second Police Witness approached the witness box and was sworn in. He confirmed his name, and that he was 16 years old. He confirmed that he was a friend of PW 1 and said he was sitting on a bench on Flixton Road with a friend when he heard shouting and saw PW 1 coming down the road towards him. His cross examination by the prosecution barrister confirmed the evidence he had given in his statement. When asked what he had done when the Police arrived he said he had walked off.

When he was cross examined by my barrister she asked him if he knew one of the youths who were prosecuted for breaking into our shed. The following is taken from court transcripts

"Yes, I don't really see him."

"Is he a friend of yours?"

"Yes. I speak to him now and again."

"Was there a time when you would hang around with him, be friends with him?"

"When I was younger."

"About what age?"

"About 13, when I used to play football with him on the green near my house."

She asked if he knew the other one of the youths prosecuted for the theft. He said that he knew him.

"I've known him all my life."

"Is he still a friend of yours?"

"Yes."

"Do you do things together?"

"No."

She now moved on to his record of criminal convictions.

"You have previous convictions, do you not?"

"Only minor convictions, it's got nothing to do with me being a witness to what I've seen."

She then went on to ask him about receiving an official warning from the police for using disorderly behaviour or threatening abusive, insulting words likely to cause harassment, alarm or distress that took place on the 14th August of the previous year, the Saturday after the incident on the Friday night. PW 2 was evasive answering, 'he couldn't remember', to most of her questions.

She questioned him about the police officers' arrival on the scene after the incident.

"You saw a car pull up, it was not a marked car?"

"Mmmm."

"The people in it shouted police at some point, did they not?"

"I can't remember."

"How did you know they were policemen?"

"Because they pulled up and started walking over to the woman. No normal people just go and start walking up to a woman with a gun, do they?"

"I am going to suggest that the reason you knew they were police is they shouted police?"

"I can't remember that."

"Why did you not stay to talk to the police?"

"Why should I?"

"You had just witnesses a serious incident, according to you?"

"Yes. It doesn't mean that I want to stay and speak to the police. I would rather go home and let them come to my house and speak to me."

"In actual fact, you did not go home, you waited on the field for —— (PW 1)".

"No, I didn't actually because I went home."

"You are saying you did not speak to —— (PW 1) later that evening or that morning?"

"I seen —— (nickname) so I was with him walking across the field. I can't remember seeing —— (PW1) because I was walking home."

"Were you present when the woman's family arrived on the field asking questions?"

"Yes, I was then."

This is when Donna and Rob had arrived and she was shouting "What have you done to my mum? She wouldn't have come out with guns for no reason!" The question which I thought the police would have asked.

She continued:

"Have you been involved in any incidents on —— —— Drive?"

"No."

"Are you aware of what I am talking about?"

"I don't even know what —— —— Drive number is."

"You know it is the address of Linda Walker and her family?"

"Yes, but how the fuck, how do I know the number."

The jury gasped in shock.

My barrister said that she had no further questions.

John's barrister now cross-examined PW 2 about John's involvement.

"The man arrived after you witnessing the pistol being discharged?"

"I seen the man coming down the road because I was stood on the other side of the road."

"At what stage?"

"At the stage when fucking —— (PW 1) and that woman were arguing."

The Judge interjected to warn him about his language.

"You describe that man as neither saying nor doing anything?"

"Yes."

"That is the truth, is it not?"

"Yes, I've just said that, I said it to this woman here."

"He was not doing anything at all?"

"He was walking down the road with a pistol, but he didn't say or do anything."

"This pistol, how far do you say you were from him when you saw that?"

"Why would I make something up?"

"I am suggesting that you are making that up to try and get him into trouble?"

"I'm saying you're making some things up to get her out of this."

"I am sorry?"

"You heard."

"I did not actually?"

"Open your ears then."

Recorder Browne said: "Just answer the questions you are being asked, not glib comments or asking counsel questions."

The barrister continued: "I am suggesting to you that you never saw the man carrying anything at all?"

"You can suggest what you want."

Recorder Browne interjected: "Did you see a man carrying a pistol?"

"Yes, I seen a man carrying a pistol."

"So you saw him, you saw something silver in his hand and you then got off?"

"Mmm, when the police pulled up here next to —— (PW 1) and her."

"Was what made you think that which was in his hand was a gun the fact that the woman was carrying guns or did it look like a gun?"

"Both; it looked like a gun and I probably though it was a gun because she's got guns in her hands shooting him. She's fucking mental. Can I go now?"

The jury gasped again and sat up in shock at his disrespect.

His poor mum was in court and even she tutted.

A statement prepared by a police officer was then read out, confirming that he had provided the DS with a tape recording of the 999 call. Both officers who attended the scene were also called to give evidence about their involvement. After this, the jury and public were dismissed whilst there were legal deliberations about presenting an exhibit from our house. It was the BB gun that John had allegedly had in his possession.

On the morning following the incident, five police officers had searched our house. When they had finished the DS asked John if there were any more weapons in the house. John had remembered that the boys used to have a BB gun when they were about fourteen. This gun fired small plastic pellets rather than ball bearings, even though it was called a BB gun.

Craig then recovered it for them from his bedroom. At this point they had no reason not to trust their intentions and were trying to co-operate as fully as possible. John was then arrested. The case put to the CPS against John had requested that he was charged with the same offences as me!

The judge decided that the gun could not be admitted as evidence unless it was first identified by PW 2, the only witness accusing John of having a gun. That night, the DS visited him at home to request that he return to court the following day to identify the gun. Apparently, PW 2 was not very co-operative. He was angry that his criminal record had been mentioned and said he had been 'treated like a criminal'. As he was 17 on 3rd February, it was no longer his parents' responsibility to ensure that he attended court and he could, and indeed he did, refuse to do so. Apparently the DS eventually won an agreement that he would attend and left. However, he did not turn up in court the following day so the gun could not be produced.

That morning, on the Thursday, before proceedings re-commenced, the prosecution barrister told the judge in closed court what PW 2 had done following the visit of the DS to his home the previous evening. Apparently, 'such was his stress' that he had 'got stoned', gone on the rampage, smashed his neighbour's window and threatened to get a shotgun to him. The police were called and PW 2 had been arrested. None of this could be disclosed in open court. The charges were still allegations at this stage. The jury would know nothing about this. Later in the year he was himself to be sent to prison for offences which included this one.

This tied up with what I later learned, that the police witnesses allegedly did not want to come to court. The police had knocked them up in the morning, almost dragged them out of bed and threatened them with conspiracy if they did not attend. PW 2 had certainly not wanted to return and had made sure that he hadn't.

I was starting to get concerned about the timescale which the judge had outlined for the trial. It was now 10.30 a.m. on Thursday and our defence had not put any evidence forward yet. I had witnesses; Donna, Rob and Craig, and John and I both had character referees who were attending. As the week progressed, it was apparent that press interest was growing. We had been on the local TV news on Tuesday and Wednesday. The case had made the national papers. More and more reporters were attending each day and the court usher had to ask them to move up to make room for the family. The prosecution continued with their case and the DS took to the stand. He and the prosecution barrister read the transcripts of our police interviews to the court. The DS was then questioned about the interview and it was time to break for lunch.

We now had only the afternoon left to present our defence, if the jury were to have Friday to deliberate their verdict. The DS approached my solicitor to ask if we were presenting any witnesses. She said that we were and he asked for their names and dates of birth so that he could check them for criminal records. When she handed over my children's details, he clutched them seemingly with glee. I was not the only one to notice this, the guard who was sitting in the dock with us also noticed. I said to her, with pride: "He won't find anything on my kids." She replied: "It's disgusting that you have to put up with this." The court staff were all very considerate towards us. One morning when I arrived at court I asked the security man on the door where all the TV cameras were, he said: "I told them they'd missed you." My dad spent half of the time wandering around the court. He couldn't hear half of what was going on but wanted to be there to support me. Needless to say, the DS found none of my children had a criminal record.

14   I Get My Say

After lunch it was my turn to take the stand. The judge, aware of the lack of time available for our defence, changed his mind about finishing on Friday. He said the jury would have to come back on Monday to give the defence a fair chance of presenting their case. The jury did not look happy, some of them shook their head and tutted. Two of the women had had their hair done. I wondered if they thought perhaps they might be on the television as the court was now packed with reporters and cameras surrounded the entrance.

I was called to the stand and the barrister for the prosecution began to question me. He had the guns on the table in front of him. The rifle was straight, not 'broken open' as it had been on the night, and the pistol was displayed in the case, organised with ammunition and gas cartridges. I felt that this was for impact on the jury. I also later found out it made the charge more serious if the gun was loaded and if ammunition was available rather than not.

The barrister slammed the empty plastic bottle which had been poured over James' car, onto a desk at the front of the court.

"This five litre plastic bottle that once contained Makro

washing up liquid was the straw that broke the camel's back, wasn't it Mrs Walker? Not a major event, to use your words, but it made you fuming mad didn't it?"

"There is no difficulty or harm in repeating it but there was no damage at all that night to the car, was there?"

"No damage at all to your house or your property?"

"The most that you lost that night was five litres of tap water, isn't that so?"

"Yes, but that front door that they split will cost £1,500 to replace."

"But that wasn't that night was it?"

I made the point that although no damage was caused on that night damage that was caused previously had run into several thousands of pounds.

"Well we may well all understand that, but those are on other occasions and as we have said, or as you have said ad infinitum in your interviews, you can't say that those people are responsible."

He continued: "What I am saying, that night it was the straw that broke the camel's back and it made you fuming mad, didn't it?"

"No, it wasn't because – what I thought that night, I was fuming mad, I was fuming mad every time anything happened. It was highly irritating and annoying and it was soul destroying when you spend your life trying to help your kids and look after your home and then someone keeps on coming around and damaging it."

"But what I was fuming mad about, was I thought: "They're here, it's actually still dripping off the bottom of the car, and it's the first time in over two years' harassment that I know they are near and I might be able to find out who they are and I might be able to get something done about it."

I felt heartened that at last I was managing to get my point across.

He said: "It is your case, if I understand it right, that you were a responsible citizen in effect trying to execute a citizen's arrest of the people that you thought were responsible, is that what you are trying to say to this jury?"

"Sort of, but I was extremely distressed and totally at the end of my tether," I replied.

He used what I had said in my interview as expressions of my shame and remorse against me;

"That you were a madwoman possessed, your words, is it true?"

"That you were absolutely fuming mad, well I think we all agree on that, don't we?"

"That you were totally off your head and totally loopy, do you agree with that?"

"I gave them a right load of 'verbals' when I walked down the street and confronted them for the first time." Is that right?"

"Yes."

"Did you do that?"

"Yes."

He went on,

"Calling them; psychos, tossers, losers, cunts, slugs." Are those the words you used?"

"I only used the C-word once when I was threatened by —— (PW 2)."

"But you used it?"

"Yes."

He continued: "Right, so you confront these youths responsible. So you think, although you agree that there is *no evidence* to support it, when you confront these youths that you think are responsible for the water bottle and what has gone on before – these youths who have placed a traffic sign at a dangerous angle in the road, youths that you are scared of – nonetheless you use those words, tossers, losers, psychos, and the like ..."

He had tried to slip in a claim that there was no evidence, as if it was a fact.

I said: "There is evidence to support it, but there is evidence."

"You weren't scared at all in truth, were you?"

"I was frightened to death." He did not understand that I was frightened but from my experience dealing with youths with behavioural problems, I knew that to show this fear would make me more vulnerable.

"There was no need first of all, was there, for you to leave your house at all that night?"

"But you said there was no evidence, there is evidence."

"Well what evidence do you suggest, just tell the jury?"

"The boys that were caught for pinching – for burgling – the shed in 2003 were friends of —— (PW 2) and in the same year at school as —— (PW 1). They were their friends."

"How does that make —— (PW 2) and —— (PW 1) in your logic ..."

"They were part of the same group."

"Does that mean that they are responsible for damaging your house?"

Did he really believe that it was a pure coincidence?

I didn't mention the proximity of PW 1 and his associate to our house, their unsavoury character or their grievances against my sons, it just seemed obvious.

He continued "Can I suggest it was within your contemplation as early as April 2004 that you were prepared to take the law effectively into your own hands and to shoot at anybody who effectively crossed your path with this weapon, isn't that right?"

"No, that's not true at all."

"So why did you say what you said in the interview?"

"Because a lot of people have a weapon in case they get burglars, it's not because you're going to shoot them, hopefully you want to deter them."

I hoped that the members of the jury, being ordinary people, would understand this personally or at least know someone who knew what it was like to feel powerless in your own home. Had we not been victimised, it would not have entered my head to have a pistol in my knicker drawer in the first place. I would have had no reason to even think of it.

The prosecution barrister then began to question me about John. I was not worried about this because I knew John had done absolutely nothing wrong. He tried to establish that John had not stopped me from going out with the weapons because he approved and was joining me even egging me on, until it was established that John had actually gone out first before me:

"Right, he made no attempt to stop you?"

"He asked me not to go out."

"But he didn't restrain you?

"John wouldn't do that, he is not violent, he wouldn't put his hands and stop somebody going ..."

"Even though you are going out with weapons ..."

"No, he asked me not to go ..."

"Right, and you ignored him ..."

"And then he went out ahead of me, the reason he went out ahead of me ... he thought if he got there first he could say, you know, "Linda, it's sorted, don't worry." He was trying to sort it before me but he went in completely the wrong direction because he set off across the field."

The barrister then turned to the transcript of my 999 call to the police.

"You say, and continue: "I have got an air rifle and I have got a pistol and I am going to shoot the fucking vandal who can come around here ...'

If your intention was not to shoot the fucking vandal why did you use the word to shoot during that conversation?"

"Because I wanted the police to come straight away, I thought if I threatened that they would be there now."

"If you had said: "I have got two guns and I am going outside to confront somebody," didn't you think that that would have the same result?"

"No, I thought they would be quicker."

"You thought they would be quicker if you used the word shoot?"

"I thought if I threatened I am going to shoot somebody ..."

"Is there any reason that you can give to the jury why it is that in that telephone conversation on the 14th of August you completely failed to request the police to come by simply explaining the truth?"

"Because they don't come."

"As you saw it?"

"They don't come."

"Someone has been damaging my house and they are at the bottom of the road?"

"It's not a priority."

"... and they are still there?"

"It's not a priority and they don't come. It's only property, it's only a car, it wasn't a lot of damage on that occasion, but they don't come."

"I am going over there now and I am going to do it." A clear indication, I suggest to you, and you can comment upon it, that to do it means to shoot, isn't that right?"

"Yes, I said I was going to go out and shoot people, yes, that's what I said."

"And you meant it, didn't you?"

"No, I didn't mean it at all. I don't go around shooting people, I just wanted to get the police to come."

After a while, he moved on to when the plain-clothed policemen arrived at the scene. They had been driving past by chance.

"The policemen who pulled up at the end, you say yourself would have been very frightened by seeing you in possession of both of these items?"

He asked if I thought that the police would be frightened how I could not think that the youths would be frightened. I said that the youths saw me as a mum of a lad their age and would have more of an idea of my character because of that. They also had more idea about why I was out with the guns, they knew what they had done to me, whereas the police officers were seeing me out of context with no knowledge of the situation but I didn't say that.

He asked me about firing to the side of ——'s (PW 1) foot,

"But did you not think it was a reckless and dangerous thing to do?"

"Well I knew it wasn't because I only fired it at the tarmac."

He then started to ask me about how I felt the police had treated my case.

"Your attitude throughout this case, Mrs Walker, has been, has it not, that the law is on the side of the yobbos', to use your words, and the criminals, not you, the victim. That's right, isn't it? That's how you think about this whole process?"

"I have felt like that, yes."

"That they have got all the rights and you have got none at all – is that how you feel?"

"I have felt like ... I do feel like that, yes."

"You took the law into your own hands that night quite deliberately?"

"Well I did phone the police."

"Armed with these weapons, didn't you?"

"Well you may say that, but I also phoned the police. I wanted the police there and if I was talking the law into my own hands I wouldn't have bothered with the police."

He had another try at John, saying: "Was your partner, Mr Cavanagh, armed with a silvery pistol that night?"

"No."

"Sure?"

"I am absolutely positive."

"Were you in a fit state to notice, bearing in mind you are upset, your anger and your temper?"

"Yes, I am absolutely positive. I swear on my children's lives. John would never, ever go out with a gun – it would be totally out of character."

"You have no right at all to behave in the way that you did, I think you agree with that, don't you?"

"I do accept that, it's not a normal ..."

"You do accept that?"

"It's not the actions of a normal person, is it, to go down the road with guns."

I was glad that he had stopped questioning me about John. I realised that swearing on my children's lives was dramatic. John later joked to me:

"Did you not want to leave any doubt about the matter?"

The fact that I said this, the strongest statement I could

imagine, reflected how strongly I felt about the lies being told about John.

He continued: "It sounds like cliché I accept but it is true, isn't it, in the early hours of the 14th of August, you acted effectively as the judge, the jury and the executioner, in relation to this, didn't you?"

I said: "No, I think that's how DS —— reacted to me actually. I think he made a case against me by going interviewing these lads before he even came and asked me. I expected to be arrested and the police say to me: "Linda, what are you doing out with them?" And then I would have said why I was out with guns. I wanted them to say ... I wanted the attention ... I wanted them to say: "What are you doing? What has driven you to the brink of your sanity that you are out with them?" And then I would have had their attention and I would be able to tell them what happened."

He asked about my teaching experience with children with emotional and behavioural difficulties and implied that I should be used to this sort of behaviour. I answered,

"The children at school usually only get themselves into that sort of state where they threaten you when they are extremely upset because something may have happened to them or something has happened in their lives to make them like that. They might be abused, very deprived and they are very, you know, they are very deprived children, some ... it's very sad. They are not just nasty. They have not turned out like that on purpose."

"Did your share of that bottle and a half of wine that night make any difference to all this, do you think?"

"No, I had two glasses of wine and that was from about six o'clock in the evening."

"When you told the police that you weren't bothered about

your own danger that was the truth, wasn't it? This is nothing to do with self-defence really, is it, this case? It is all about your temper, I suggest, isn't that right?"

"Well I was ... I was in a temper, but wouldn't most people be in a temper especially when people start on their children?"

"I have no further questions," he said.

It was now my barrister's chance to re-examine me, picking up on any points which had been raised that she believed needed to be clarified.

She said: "You have been asked about your temper and why you took the guns out. I think it is accepted by everyone, you never aimed the gun ... well, you never aimed the gun at —— (PW 1) did you?"

"No, never pointed ... well, I pointed it towards ... at his foot, when he was toe to toe with me then moved it away."

"Did you at any point try to shoot —— (PW 1)?"

"No, never."

"Did you at any point try to shoot any of the others?"

"No."

"If you had wanted to shoot them could you have?"

"Oh yes, I could have done, I was well within the range."

"And it has been put to you that you did all this through temper, do you accept that?"

"No, I was in a bad temper obviously, I was extremely angry and I was in a bad temper, but I was in a bad temper because of what they had done and they were coming starting yet another weekend on vandalising yet another one of my children's cars."

"And you have said repeatedly that you wanted the police there, is that correct?"

"Yes."

Our legal team and were pleased with how I presented my evidence. They thought I had managed to get my case across well. On the strength of this, they decided not to call my witnesses Donna, her fiancé Rob and Craig, believing it unnecessary. By this time, the third day of the trial was over and the court was adjourned until the following day. When we left the court, Donna received a text message from a colleague, saying that one of our pupils who did a paper round had seen me on the front page of the Manchester Evening News. Now half of the school knew why I was off and that is was not because I was ill, as they assumed. The staff had told them not to mention this to anyone as it might mean I could not return. So they were all keeping quiet and pretending they didn't know, which I found really touching. I received a text message from the only girl in the school. She text: "Miss we hope you get not guilty we know you are not guilty we luv you x". It made me upset. I realised how much I was missing them, even though they could be a handful at times. I also knew that I was important to them, some of them in particular.

15   John Doesn't Keep a Loaded Weapon

On Friday morning, it was John's turn to be grilled. He was very nervous and stressed before taking the stand. John does not look good when he is stressed, he goes very red – probably due to his high blood pressure – and sweats. I was still confident though that his genuine, non-violent and gentle nature would come through.

The barrister asked a wide range of questions:

"What did you think when she started picking up these weapons?"

"I thought that what she was doing was inappropriate."

"What did you think she was going to do?"

"I thought she was going to do exactly what she did do, which was to put her on the same standing as the boys. In other words, they were intimidating her and she wanted to even the odds."

"Did she tell you she was going to shoot them?"

"No, I don't believe she did. I think I only heard that when I passed her as she was making a phone call."

"So why not take them off her at that point?"

"I would physically have had to take them off her and I wasn't going to fight her for them."

"Is it because you acquiesced and agreed with what she was doing?"

"No. I wasn't in agreement with what she was doing."

"There was nothing to physically prevent you disarming her, but you simply chose not to do so, is that what you are saying to the jury?"

"I chose not to do so. What I did choose to do was tell her to phone the police and what I chose to do was go out ahead of her."

"You heard her, when she was on the phone, saying to the police that she was going to shoot people?"

"I did hear her say that, yes."

"Did that not cause you to pause and to think?"

"It caused me to make haste onto the field."

"When you heard these words, did you not believe her; she sounded serious on the tape?"

"No. I didn't believe Linda would shoot anybody."

"So why did you think she was saying that to the police?"

"Because she wanted the police there."

He moved on to the gun.

"Why was this pistol in the knicker drawer in the bedroom?"

"Because Linda wanted it there."

"Why?"

"Because of all the problems that we had had over a period of time."

"Why did Linda want it there?"

"She wanted it there because it gave her some comfort to have it there."

"Who loaded the gun for her?"

"The gun wasn't loaded, to my belief."

"So she has loaded it that night?"

"Linda wouldn't have a clue how to load the gun."

"So who loaded it; one of you has?"

"No. It has a gas canister in it."

"There were pellets in the magazine?"

"There were no pellets in the magazine."

"So you are saying that, when this pistol was taken out, no pellets were discharged at all because there were no pellets in it in the first place?"

"I don't believe there were any pellets in that pistol."

"When had you last checked this pistol?"

"It was some time previously; maybe three months."

"In what circumstances?"

"I think it was probably when Linda wanted it in the knicker drawer."

"Do you remember specifically checking it?"

"I don't remember specifically checking it."

"Would you not automatically check it; if you are bringing this pistol into the bedroom ..."

"Yes, precisely."

"... knowing what it is going to be used for?"

"I don't keep a loaded weapon; I can be fairly certain that there were no pellets in it, because I don't keep a loaded weapon. Linda may have thought it was."

"Does Linda know how to load this weapon?"

"No, she wouldn't have an idea."

"Was that not part of the lessons?"

"No, it wasn't."

"But you did give her lessons and instructions in how to use the weapons?"

"She said: "How to you fire it?" I said: "You pull the trigger." I told her you have to take the safety catch off."

"Did you have target practice with her?"

"No.

He questioned John about the allegation that he also went out with a gun.

"Is not the reality that you did take a silver pistol out with you?"

"Absolutely not."

"But you had it in your hand?"

"I did not have a pistol."

"The conduct of both of you that night was wholly inappropriate?"

"I think Linda had been pushed over the limit."

"You encouraged her to go out in those circumstances?"

"I absolutely did not encourage her, no."

"You were mad and angry yourself?"

"I was not mad and angry."

"You were certainly mad and angry enough to stand in front of —— (PW1) and lie to him and say that you had seen him interfering with property?"

"I don't think that's mad and angry; I was testing somebody. You're testing me now. I felt I had the right to test him."

"I do it, with respect, with an element of courtesy, I hope; you were shouting and screaming in his face, were you not?"

"I was courteous."

"Were you shouting and screaming in his face?"

"Absolutely not. I don't believe I was speaking to him in a voice that is more raised than it is now and I am stressed, yes, and I probably was then."

The barrister asked John regarding taking guns out onto the street.

"Would you say that is taking the law into your own hands?"

"No, I don't. I don't think, under the circumstances, Linda

was taking the law into her own hands. I think she wanted to defend herself, I think what she wanted to do was put herself on the same level as those youths that were challenging her; that's what I believe."

Despite repeated questioning and having accusations thrown at him, John never raised his voice once. He had remained polite and respectful throughout. I would have been shocked if he had done anything else as John is a gentleman who very rarely loses his composure. I hoped that this would show the jury that even under significant pressure, as we had been on the night of the incident, John still remained calm and polite. John was not capable of causing an affray. His gentle nature was also the reason he had not tried to restrain me, going out himself first to try to resolve the conflict, rather than the accusation he approved of my actions. He had stated clearly that he did not approve. I hoped that the jury would recognise his true character from listening to his evidence.

16   Facts and Fantasies

Our defence team then presented our character witnesses to the court. I had six written references and John had four. John's colleague Stephen Pendlebury attended court to give his reference under oath as did my friend Susan Curtis, also Nigel Haslam, my ex head teacher from school, the one who had appointed me. Susan described me as a "mother hen who looked after everybody". Mr Haslam told the court of Ofsted's praise for my work and how it had been held up as good practice. The written references, which have been referred to earlier, were also passed to the judge. After our witnesses gave evidence and our written references were read out, the prosecution barrister was asked if he had any questions for the witnesses. He said he did not and hung down his head, he looked like a beaten man. Our character referees had done us proud. It was obvious that to try to discredit them would be futile.

Only the barristers' closing speeches now remained. There were now ten reporters in the small court. The prosecution barrister addressed the jury with his closing speech first.

"As members of the public, you are brought here to see that justice is done."

He raised the issue of householders rights and their right

to defend themselves, "There has been, you will be aware, a good deal of debate in recent times regarding the rights of in particular of householders to attack, or even kill, intruders in defence of their own home and we are all encouraged, are we not, if you think about it, to be aware of the limits of self defence. You know that people risk prosecution only if they step over the line, the line that separates self defence from retribution and revenge. It is not self defence, after all, if you are an attacker – if you carry out an attack – then you cannot rely upon self defence and that is simple common sense.

He continued: "The law regarding self defence has not changed. If you are attacked, or if you are in fear of being about to be attacked, a person is entitled to use reasonable force in self defence.

Regarding householders rights to defend their home and property he used a series of so-called 'Cluedo guidelines' to illustrate this.

"Mrs White disturbs a burglar in the library, he flees empty handed, she chases after him and shoots him dead with a shotgun. Lawful or unlawful, obviously unlawful, wholly out of proportion, even if the burglar did bring the situation upon himself and so it goes on. One final example, even closer to the situation we find ourselves in here. Reverend Green hears a rumour that somebody is going to steal from his car, so, instead of phoning the police, or having phoned the police, he lies in wait for the thief and, when the thief comes by, as he breaks into the vehicle, he kills him. Unlawful because it is disproportionate, the intruder has not asked to be dealt with in that way and nor does he deserve it. He could have called the police, he could have let the police deal with the situation. After all, it was only a car theft, the force used was wholly disproportionate in those circumstances." How he could say this example was "even closer to the situation we find ourselves in here" I do not know, no one having even been hurt let alone killed!

He applied this directly to the case then, saying: "My submission to you is that common sense dictates (and the law says too) that self defence does not apply here, it does not even get off the ground. You cannot take guns out into a public street, knowing that they are loaded, hoping that you do not have to use them, but use them nevertheless when the person that you are confronting is unarmed."

He continued: "I submit to you that she plainly overstepped the mark – she overstepped that line between self defence, retribution and revenge – and, what is more, she did so knowing what she had said to the police on the telephone and you cannot overstep that line."

He also addressed the criminal convictions of the police witnesses, that their convictions were for the same sort of offences that we were accusing them of committing at our house, he said,

"but what you cannot do is to use the convictions of —— (PW 1) and —— (PW 2) to in some way prove the fact that they were responsible for the campaign, if it was a campaign, the incidents of damage and nuisance at ——— ——— Drive, because those convictions prove absolutely nothing at all."

He concluded by saying: "Of course they are people of good character (His Honour will give you the appropriate direction), but it is not a passport to acquittal, particularly not in a case like this. Even the biggest baddest villain, the worst armed robber, the worst murderer, starts with a good character. Some people keep their good character all their lives, others, sadly, lose them along the way and these two lost it in August last year.

He went on to say, "the only proper, safe, fair and true

verdicts in this case are verdicts of guilty, in relation to both defendants, on each count they face. "Your Honour, those are my submissions to the jury. Ladies and gentlemen, thank you for your attention."

My barrister then made her closing speech in my defence, delving into fine points of law to prove that not guilty verdicts were appropriate.

"The main part of the offence we are challenging is unlawful violence; that Linda Walker on that day had those two air weapons with her in order to cause unlawful violence – she did not – and that was the bottom line, we say in this case.

"The crown's case (count 1) is wholly dependent on them proving that, when she went out with those weapons, it was with intent to cause those boys to fear unlawful violence would be used against them and that is the heart of Linda Walker's defence case. While that is true for count 1, the unlawfulness of her behaviour goes to the heart of count 2 as well, because you will recall what is required for an affray is that the person is required to use or threaten unlawful violence and we say again she did not use it – she did not threaten unlawful violence – and that is the key here."

She challenged the prosecution's assertion that a 'not guilty' verdict would be a mandate for others to take to the streets with guns.

She went on to look at the case in three stages. Firstly, Stage 1: how the incident started and my reaction to it. The gallon container on the car, the water still dripping, and how I went out.

"Members of the Jury, she does not nip upstairs and get her air weapon, saying: "Right, that's it, I've had enough, I'm going to teach them a lesson." She just goes out into the street, in her lilac pants, and her lilac top and her flip flops, she is unarmed, she had no intention of being a vigilante, she has not been pushed over the edge, she is just going to see if they are nearby. She has had enough, but she wants to see whether she can finally spot the people who have been doing this."

She then went on to Stage 2: me going out with the weapons.

"First of all, the Crown seek to use the fact that she has got this rifle as helpful to them. We say the opposite. If her intention at that point was to shoot anybody, why take a rifle with nothing in it, where the butt at the front is broken down and there is no evidence, certainly not from the civilian witnesses, that she made any attempt to either load that rifle or put the butt up. Why does someone take a rifle out with them that is empty, if their intent is to shoot somebody; no, her intention at that point was to scare the boys, but we say it was a lawful intention. The only reason she wanted to scare those boys was to deter them from threatening her or threatening her home; a deterrent; put them off doing anything to her while she was waiting for the police. Both of those things, we say, are lawful behaviour."

She continued: "Why did she phone the police? And I accept she does sound distressed (we all remember the tape), she does sound deeply upset but she has had enough."

"We say it is a cry for help."

"She repeatedly says in her interview and in her evidence to you yesterday: "I just wanted them there now.""

"What do we know about the boys? We know that they are acquaintances and certainly —— (PW 2) is a friend, a good friend, he has known him all his life, of the boys who are responsible for the shed burglary back in 2003, we know that for a fact because it was put to the witness and, while —— (PW 1) said he knew one of them as an acquaintance,

—— (PW 2) said one was someone he had known all his life and was a friend of his. Again, it does not mean they did it (the prosecution are quite right) but here we are not here to prove that they were involved, we are simply here to say she thought they were, she thought they were involved because of their proximity to the incident and because she had seen what they had done with the road sign."

She continued: "The Crown say she went out to shoot them, it was revenge, it was retribution, it was not self-defence. Members of the jury, if Linda Walker had wanted to shoot those boys, she could have and she would have and she did not and that, I say, speaks volumes. If the Crown are really suggesting that she was a vigilante and she had had enough, why did she not shoot them?

Then we have the evidence of the police that, as soon as they identify themselves as police officers and say put it down, she puts it down. She is not interested in anything else, she just wanted the police there, and then we have heard she is carted off and she is shouting, she says (and it is accepted by —— (PW 1), but not the police): "Why are you arresting me not him?" And then it is accepted by everybody that she makes this comment about her MP. It sounds like a silly comment in the context of everything that has happened but we say it shows her state of mind, that all of this is to do with the incidents at her home, all of this is not revenge or retribution, it is the fact she feels under threat, her family is under threat, her home is under threat, her partner is under threat. In her interview, when she is talking about her children, that is when she starts crying, "it is when they try to take your children's things," she says, "that it really gets you," and she starts crying. In her evidence yesterday, you might think when she talks about the way her partner will not let things out, but instead he suffers angina and chest pains, all of these events, members of the jury, have a deep effect on Linda Walker and all she was trying to do on that day was to make sure they did not happen again and in her mind that was her intent – to stop things happening again – but lawfully, by getting the police there, by stopping these boys from threatening her, that is all she wanted to do."

John's barrister also made a closing speech, casting doubt in particular on the evidence of —— (PW 2), who claimed John had a gun.

With the closing speeches made, Recorder Browne said that he would adjourn for the weekend and give his summing up on Monday. After the jury were dismissed, the Judge told all three barristers that in his summing up he intended to tell the jury that "these poor people have had a terrible time", and that "where there is a conflict of evidence to believe and take account of the defendants' good character against the dubious character of the witnesses". I thought this sounded very positive.

17   The Family Close Ranks

We arrived in court at 10 a.m. on the Monday morning to find the court full of reporters. There were ten again and the family struggled to find a seat. The judge started his summing up, which went on for about an hour. It seemed very fair. He gave the jury some legal advice and asked them to consider which law, if any, had been broken. He also went into detail on the law of self defence. Finally, he said that if they had any doubt about whether we were guilty, they must return a not guilty verdict. The onus of proof was on the prosecution rather than the defence. When I later read the transcript of his summing up, it was ten pages long; the first two and a half pages related to the law, six pages followed which gave a summary of the evidence as presented equally by both sides. His summary of the closing speeches given by the three barristers, took up: the prosecution barrister one paragraph, my barrister: three paragraphs, and John's barrister: two paragraphs. Five paragraphs to us and one to the prosecution.

When he had finished the summary, he said: "Members of the Jury, you must reach, if you can, a unanimous verdict on the two counts that you have to consider. As you may know, the law allows me in certain circumstances to accept a verdict which is not the verdict of you all. Those circumstances have not arisen, so when you retire, I ask you to reach a verdict on which each one of you is agreed. Should, however, the time come when I can accept a majority verdict, I shall call you back into court and give you a further direction. When you retire, please choose one of your number to be your spokesperson and to chair your deliberations. Please take with you the exhibits."

We were quite pleased with this although it gave the jury little direction. We did not feel we had been proven guilty and this gave us hope. The witnesses were known criminals and had convictions for the type of offences that had been committed against us. We assumed we would be believed, rather than them, since we knew we were telling the truth and they were not. The jury were sent out at 10.52 a.m. and we went to sit in the foyer. My son James turned up with his girlfriend, unable to concentrate at work. He had felt compelled to be with us, bless him.

The waiting was extremely boring and I was apprehensive. If I was found guilty I worried I would almost certainly lose my job. I did not believe however that anyone would want to send me to prison. My character references had painted me to be an angel, I had no previous convictions, I had always been a good citizen.

After an hour or so we were called back in. My barrister told me it was only for a point of law, rather than a verdict. The jury wanted some clarification on the law from the judge because they had not understood. The prosecution had said that our combined actions had caused an affray and the jury wanted to know if that meant they had to find us both guilty or not guilty together. The answer did not seem very clear to me but I think my brain was overloaded by that point. We waited again and nothing happened for several hours. My solicitor said it was a good sign if the jury took a long time as it meant they could not agree and if they were not sure, they had to go with not guilty. At 3 p.m. we were called back in. I was told by my barrister: "Prepare yourself, it is for a verdict."

The foreman of the jury was asked had they reached a verdict on the count of affray alleged against John. He said: "Yes." Had they reached a verdict on both counts alleged against me? "No." He was then asked for the verdict on the count against John. "Not guilty." I squeezed John's hand and he said: "Thank God" and gave a sigh of relief. At that point he had to leave me to go and sit in the public gallery. I felt lonely and vulnerable sat in the dock now without John. I said to the nice lady guard: "At least he can keep me in idle luxury." I knew that at least his job was now safe, which was a relief. If John had been found guilty, I dread to think what would have become of us.

The judge then gave the jury a majority direction, which meant they didn't all have to agree on the charges against me. He was willing to accept a majority verdict. We were then dismissed to sit in the foyer again, with the ten reporters. My barrister said that if no verdict could be reached by the end of the day, the judge may dismiss the jury and declare a mistrial. That would mean the case may be dropped or there could be a retrial if requested by the police and ordered by the judge. At 4.30 p.m. we were called back into court. I was told to prepare myself, which made me feel like I was going to be hanged, it was for a verdict.

The judge asked if the jury had reached a unanimous decision. The foreman said: "No". The judge asked: "Have you reached a majority decision?" The foreman answered: "Yes."

The judge said: "On the charge of affray have you reached a verdict?"

"Yes."

"On the charge of possession of firearms with intent to cause fear of unlawful violence, have you reached a verdict?"

"No."

"What is your verdict on the charge of Affray?"

"Guilty."

I was determined not to give anyone the satisfaction of looking upset. I didn't know what my reaction was, I was stunned. I just stood there and did not move or change my expression whatsoever. I was still hopeful. I thought: "They don't want to find me guilty on count one, they've found me guilty on count two because I did do something." This verdict was rather worrying though because my barrister had said in her summing up that if they couldn't find me guilty on count one, they could not find me guilty on count two either, since both counts relied on the same premise – that the violence threatened was unlawful. This I assumed was because she thought she had convinced the jury that count one could not be proven. The verdict had come in at a 10–2 majority. I had thought all along that the police had brought this charge as a back-up to the firearms charge to increase their chances of 'getting a result'.

The judge said that we would adjourn for the day and apologised as he told the jury that we must reconvene on the following day. They really shook their heads and tutted this time. They were not happy. They were supposed to have been dismissed on Friday. I think that by now they had really had enough. As I left the court, I was crowded by reporters. My son James tried to stand between me and them and ended up barging into a camera. It was all quite unnerving. They wanted me to comment but I knew that if I said something, it would make it more difficult in relation to my job. I could be accused

The tree-lined road in suburban Manchester where the incident took place and the actual road sign, photographed on 16th August 2004.

A Walther CP88 Gas Powered Air Pistol.

The wall where the youths were as they chanted 'Linda and John' threateningly.

Above: 'Free Linda' Campaigners outside HMP Styal 10th April 2005.
Below: Petition presented by campaigners with Bev Hughes to Paul
Goggins, Minister for Prisons 30th April 2005.

(Pictures courtesy of *Manchester Evening News*.)

Above: Home Awaits 4th May 2005. *Below*: Arriving Home.

(Pictures courtesy of *Manchester Evening News*.)

Above: Prison cell pictures, these kept me sane.
Below: At home with the petition of 10,000 plus signatures and some letters and cards.

of bringing the school into disrepute by volunteering to speak to the media, so I kept quiet.

When we arrived back in court on Tuesday, the jury was sent out immediately. The previous night had been difficult for all of us. We were obviously relieved that John had been found not guilty but I felt apprehensive having had one guilty verdict delivered. Again we waited in the foyer. Sue Ann said if it went on much longer, it would be a mistrial. If by 11.30 a.m. no decision had come back from the jury, the judge had agreed to accept no verdict. At 11.12 a.m. after six hours and 35 minutes of deliberation, the jury came back with a verdict.

I was again told to prepare myself and went back into the dock alone. The foreman was asked if they had reached a verdict and he said they had. The judge then asked if they had reached a unanimous verdict. To my surprise, the foreman replied: "Yes." I thought it must be not guilty because they could not even all agree on the Affray, and that was a lesser count. The judge asked for the verdict.

"Guilty."

I was totally stunned. I felt numb. The judge seemed shocked as well and the whole court fell completely silent. I was determined to keep completely composed. If they had taken so long to reach a verdict, there must have been doubts and if there were doubts they were supposed to come to a not guilty verdict. Everyone is innocent until proven guilty. The judge had stated this clearly in his summing up. All these thoughts went through my head as I stood there. It felt unreal to me. I felt a stubborn determination not to show how shell-shocked I really felt. I thought: "What can they do to me? If they send me to prison, I'll still get my tea and be able to watch Coronation Street." I also felt defiant, that after all the media coverage, if they did imprison me, there would be an outcry. I thought: "If they want to send me to prison let them do it and let them take the consequences, if they're brave enough!"

The judge said: "All sentencing options remain open." They discussed dates for sentencing and settled on 23rd March, three weeks away. He requested pre-sentence reports be prepared. I was then allowed to leave and went into an interview room with Sue Ann and my barrister. They said that although prison was a possibility, the preparation of pre-sentence reports indicated that he was considering a community order. I said: "I'm not doing community service." I thought: "They can get stuffed". I felt I had helped people all my life and this was how I was being repaid. I was annoyed.

My barrister said: "Don't say that because that will increase the risk of you going to prison." John did not want me to go to prison so I agreed to keep my options open.

I then went out to find my family. I felt terrible seeing my children so upset and I tried to put a brave face on it for their sakes. When we arrived home, friends and family were ringing constantly, as well as the press. The news had been announced on the radio and television before we had even left the court. I put a message on the answer machine saying: "Hi, this is Linda. Thank you for your support. We are too busy to come to the phone right now, but please leave your number and I will get back to you."

I could hear the messages as they were being left so that I could selectively pick up the phone. Some messages were upsetting. Old friends rang, some of whom were crying. I took down the numbers of the journalists from newspapers, magazines, TV and radio, and kept them in a pad. I didn't want to talk to them at that time because my barrister had told me it could adversely affect my sentence, but I thought I may want to at some time in the future.

I had to go out as I needed some shopping so I went to Somerfield in Urmston. I felt terrible, paranoid that everyone would recognised me from being on television all week. I felt shamed to death even though I knew I had not done anything to harm to anyone. I felt stressed and my heart was pounding. When I got home I took one of the tablets the doctor had prescribed for me when James' car had been broken into in December and I had suffered an anxiety attack. I was trying to be strong but was now struggling.

I decided to do something positive so I wrote to the Home Secretary. In my letter I told him that if I hadn't removed the road sign things could be very different now, I could be a witness at a manslaughter trial! I also wrote a letter to my neighbours in our Drive explaining the situation. Some of them had been interviewed by the press. When the media visited every house in our road, everyone had either made no comment or supported my action. I thanked them for that support. Some had also sent letters of support, cards and even a prayer.

18   Outrage and Outcry

The following day, the local BBC radio station GMR had a phone-in on the Alan Beswick programme. The subject was: "What sentence should Linda get?" The responses included many entertaining answers, like: 'a holiday to recuperate', 'a medal' and 'target practice!' Some gave advice like: "She should have invited them in for a nice cup of tea and then shot them." These people were sticking up for me and understood how I had felt. They knew that what I had done was over the top and were using their sense of humour to reflect this. They understood, empathised with my distress and that meant a lot to me.

The DS was interviewed on the show. He said there was no evidence that these were the youths that had been to our house, that they were 250 yards down the road when I found them, and that there was no damage or anything stolen that night, etc. I rang the following morning to ask for a recording of the show. I wanted it as evidence for my police complaint. I was told that the switchboard had been jammed during the phone-in. They said they had never had so many people trying to get through for a phone-in, which demonstrated the strength of feeling for the issues that were raised. It made me feel a lot better; comforted by the knowledge that people did not think I was an evil and terrible person.

After the trial, my friends and family were angry at the jury. I do not blame members of the jury individually. They were persuaded by a very experienced and charismatic prosecution barrister and were influenced by his theatrical dramatics. They knew as I did that I had done something I shouldn't have done. However I thought perhaps they had not fully grasped the gravity of the charges. People tend to think that there is no smoke without fire and the jury probably felt that because I went out with guns, I must be guilty and that I wouldn't be in the Crown Court in the first place if I hadn't done something serious. It was still most odd after only coming to a majority decision on the lesser charge to suddenly, when they didn't want to be called back for a further day, come to a unanimous decision on the more serious charge. I and many others couldn't understand how this could happen. Surely you would expect that the decision they were in agreement on would come first and the one in dispute would come later, not the other way round!

I received many cards and letters from old friends, some from people I had not heard from for years. My special friends, 'the girls', got me a lovely bouquet. It had a card, which read: "Remember us when you're famous!" I drew strength from the support of everyone and my family were proud of me. I wrote to Cherie Blair and sent her a copy of my letter to the Home Secretary. I wrote to her because I knew that she was a barrister. I didn't know if the letter would even reach her but it was better than sitting around and feeling sorry for myself. I did get an acknowledgement back saying that Mrs Blair could not comment on legal matters. I also got a telephone call from a probation officer who wanted me to attend an interview for the pre-sentence report and I made an appointment with her.

On Thursday, 10th February, 2005 – two days after I had been found guilty – I was at my friend Barbara's house with 'the girls' for our usual weekly meeting. We have a drink and chat and generally catch up with each other's news. When I arrived home, John said the milkman had been and had told him that he had seen PW 1 and two others at our house when we were away in April 2004. He said he had seen them once in the evening and another time at around 5.30 a.m., running away suspiciously from our back garden. We were quite shocked at this revelation. We realised that this could prove the case made against us was based on a false premise. April was when our shed had been burgled, when we were away at our caravan for Easter. I sent Sue Ann a text, thinking that she would get it first thing in the morning. Sure enough, she rang early on. She sounded excited. She told me not to get my hopes up but that this was 'new evidence' and could therefore provide grounds for an appeal against the conviction. I was quite excited about this news, John was not so positive. His enthusiasm now dampened by cynicism. I had been instructed not to speak to the milkman myself as this could be seen as 'coercion'. Instead, we were to ask him to ring her.

I rang the dairy that supplied our milk and said that I needed to contact David our milkman, as soon as possible. He rang me that afternoon and agreed to ring my solicitor. After that, apart from when he came to collect his milk money on a Thursday, I did not speak to him about it directly again. Things must have moved quickly after he spoke to the solicitor. The police called him in to make a statement. That happened on the following Tuesday, 15th February, 2005, and Sue Ann called me to let me know that it was going to take place.

I was worried because his evidence challenged the case against me. I asked Sue Ann: "Could he not give the written statement to you to pass to them instead?" She said he had to be interviewed by the police in person but that she knew what his evidence was after speaking on the phone to him and if his statement was significantly different, they would be asking why. I did not want the DS in charge of the case taking Mr Mathews statement following the grossly exaggerated version of events that had been contained in court papers from the CPS. I was worried he may try to discredit it. Sue Ann conveyed my concerns and it was agreed that another officer, who was impartial to the case, would take Mr Mathews statement and we later received a copy.

In it he said, "On the 18th January 2005 I went away with my family for two weeks to the Dominican Republic, returning on Wednesday 2nd February 2005. I returned to work the following day."

He continued: "The following week, Linda seemed to be in the newspapers and on the television daily. Reports were being given on the trial on either the 8th or 9th February 2005. I remember seeing the news on television and again it was reporting news on Linda's case. It stated that she had been found guilty and faced up to ten years in prison. I then realised how serious this was and heard people via the news offering support to Linda. I mentioned to my wife about seeing the boys including —— (PW 1) at Linda's house last year and I asked her if she thought I should take this to come forward with the information. I did not know who or what to do or where to go to with the information. I did not even know if it would be of any importance. I therefore decided to go and tell Linda, so I went to her house on Thursday 10th February 2005. Linda was not at home so I spoke with her partner John. I told him that early in 2004 around April time, I had seen —— (PW 1) and two unknown males around 20.30 hours in their Avenue. I remember it being a Thursday as I was collecting. I remember they were acting suspiciously and hiding near some tress near to Linda and John's. —— (PW 1) had a baseball cap on, but the other two had hoods up so I couldn't see their faces. I recognised —— (PW 1) and asked what they were up to, they said they were either at or waiting for their mates, pointing to Linda and John's. I didn't think anything more of this. I also told him the Saturday morning following this about 05.30 hours, whilst I was delivering milk at ——— ——— Drive. I saw —— (PW 1) and again two mates who I don't know running off and away from Linda and John's driveway. I again asked what they were up to, they said something like they were just going. I again thought nothing of this as I knew Linda and John were away and presumed they had been with their son, as I again presumed he had remained at home."

He continued: "I felt stuck in the middle as I know two parties involved, but felt I had to come forward and pass on the information although as I've stated I do not know if this will help in any way. I am a willing police witness and will attend at Court to give evidence as stated if required. I would like to add that when I spoke with John, I told him I know —— (PW 1) had been in trouble in the past but I know since then he has worked hard and is a good lad from a decent family. I even went to his parent's wedding a couple of years ago."

The prosecution had made such a big deal about these not being the youths who had been coming to our house and had stated repeatedly there was no evidence whatsoever that would indicate otherwise. PW 1 under oath in his evidence to the court had clearly denied that he had ever been to my house as an invited or uninvited guest except on one occasion.

We believed that this provided clear grounds for a charge of perjury against PW 1. We waited for a decision from the CPS.

A charge of perjury would greatly assist my case for appeal. I was very hopeful. The evidence was clear and as far as we could see, could not be contradicted. My barrister decided to wait for the decision before putting in an application to appeal. We waited and we waited. It had taken ten days between the incident and the police charging myself and John. Ten days came and went. I had been convicted on 8th February and we had one month to lodge an appeal from that date. The application had to be at the appeal courts in London by 8th March, 2005, at the latest.

Two weeks and six days later, on the 7th March, 2005, there was still no decision. At 4 p.m. that day, I received a call from Sue Ann. She said the application for leave to appeal, which means permission from the judge to appeal, had gone in. She said: "It has gone to the Royal Court of Justice on the Strand in London". My barrister had decided that we had sufficient grounds to apply even without the perjury charge. Hopefully it would be forthcoming before we got to appeal. I was thrilled by this as my barrister was very cautious and I thought that if she believed we already had grounds, our case would be strengthened greatly once the charge of perjury was brought against PW 1. Surely any trial in which it is proved that the main witness did not tell the truth must be a mistrial. John tempered my excitement with his caution and disillusionment, saying: "Don't get your hopes up Linda. They all piss in the same pot and they don't want to help you." It was very unusual for John to swear and an indication of his frustration at my predicament.

The day after our appeal application was lodged, our milkman David Matthews was contacted again by the police. They said they needed to clarify a few points in his statement, and could they call at his house and have a meeting with him. So on Wednesday, 9th March, two police officers visited him and his wife. They asked some very negative questions about his statement. They asked:

How, if it was 5.30 a.m., he could see them because it would have been dark?

Why was he delivering milk if he knew we were away?

Why had he not come forward earlier?

If he saw them running away from the garden, did that mean he had not actually seen them inside the garden?

Could he explain exactly how he thought they were acting 'suspiciously'?

Mr Matthews answered their questions as fairly as he could and we later received a copy of his statement. He said that he was unable to confirm the exact dates when he saw the youths at our house and whether we were away. He said it could have been that we were away for the weekend but he had been told that deliveries were to continue as usual for the rest of the family. He said that he specifically remembered the incident at night taking place on a Thursday as that was the day he always collected his money in that area. Although he had recognised PW 1 he confirmed that PW 2 was not one of the other two.

He also said that the second incident happened at 5.30 a.m. on the following Saturday.

"I initially saw nothing untoward and alighted from the float delivering to the address in the corner. I then returned to my float at which point I had my float to my left and Linda's house was to my right hand side. It was at this point that I saw three males running out of the driveway of the house. I first saw them about half way along the driveway almost immediately I recognised the males as the same ones I had seen the Thursday before and I recognised —— (PW 1) as being one of them. Again it was dark but the area was well lit by street lighting and I believe that there is a street light immediately outside the address. As the males passed me they were no more than 10 yds away at the closest point all were wearing hooded tops with hoods over their heads and it was over in a matter of seconds. I actually saw —— (PW 1)'s face and the other male who I don't know his name and I am happy it was them that ran away from the address. Again none of the males were in possession of any property as they left as far as I could tell."

He continued: "I was surprised to see —— (PW 1) and the males at that time in the morning and it did arise my suspicions. I did think about knocking at the house to make enquiries but I didn't because I believed Linda and John were away for the weekend and it may have been the lads had been visiting the address innocently as I know in the past the children at the address have had parties when their parents were away. I decided that I would leave it and see if anything was mentioned the following weeks. Nothing was mentioned and I dismissed the incident as irrelevant."

Mr Matthews was clearly a credible witness, an upstanding citizen who knew the family of the youth and had nothing to gain by coming forward. I later found out that although the investigating DS did not personally take the statements, he was still fully in charge of the investigation. When our solicitor had raised my concerns and been told another officer would be tasked with taking the statement apparently a Superintendent had intervened and asserted that, 'the DS's integrity was beyond reproach' and he would conduct the investigation! I thought 'invalidate' rather than 'clarify' his statement would have been a better description of what took place.

PW 1 was never interviewed regarding our allegation of

perjury or for any of the implications of Mr Mathews statement. Even though this was the weekend at Easter – the only weekend in April that we went away, when our shed was burgled and an attempt was made to break into our home. We were away from the Wednesday evening prior to the Bank Holiday weekend until the Bank Holiday Monday. My daughter Donna and her fiancé Rob had joined us at the caravan.

19   Waiting for Sentencing

I had a meeting with a probation officer. The job of a probation officer is to assess the most appropriate methods for dealing with criminals in order to protect the public. She asked me about the incident and I explained exactly what had happened. She asked me what I would do if they came back again. I said: "I keep a flash camera loaded with batteries and film handy" and I told her that I would go out and take their picture so I had evidence to show to the police. She suggested I considered not going out at all.

At the end of the interview she went through the options for sentencing. They were custody, community service, electronic tagging, a home detention curfew, or a probation order. She said she was going to recommend that prison would be highly inappropriate for me. Community service she said, might involve something like working in a charity shop, but she was not going to recommend this either – probably because I had worked for the community all my working life. She thought tagging or a curfew were also inappropriate. Instead, she informed me she was going to recommend probation, which involved regular meetings with a probation officer along with attending a 'Think First' program, which was a sort of anger management therapy.

She said she would be looking at my character references and psychiatric report before she completed her report, which I knew were very positive. About a month after the meeting, she gave me a call to ask me to come to see her again on 14th March, before the sentencing. I asked if anything was wrong but she said not. She just wanted to check everything before she submitted her report. I wondered whether she was perhaps taking extra care because the case was now so high profile.

Prior to Easter 2005, about three or four weeks after I had sent my letter to the Home Secretary, I had not received a reply to my letter to the Home Office. I had telephoned to ask if it had been received. I explained to the receptionist that I had not received any acknowledgement and she transferred me to the correspondence department but my call went to answer machine. I tried several times unsuccessfully and eventually asked if I could speak to a real person. I was passed through to the Right Honourable Charles Clark's personal secretary. I told him who I was and started to explain why I had telephoned. To my surprise, he knew who I was straight away and said that the Home Secretary was dealing with my case personally. He was taking advice on the law of self defence and would be writing to me within 20 days. I was surprised that my letter was considered so important to be handled at such a high level but I was also heartened.

I received a reply from the Home Office from Baroness Scotland, on behalf of the Home Secretary prior to going away to our caravan for Easter. She said,

"I would like to reassure you that this Government takes the problem of anti-social behaviour very seriously. That is why we have introduced local crime and disorder reduction partnerships under the Crime and Disorder Act 1998. These enable the police, local authorities and other agencies representing the

local community to work together to identify the crime and disorder problems in their area and ensure that strategies are in place for tackling them. She gave some guidelines on what constituted the charges I had been convicted of and confirmed the sentences of 7 and 3 years respectfully <u>and</u> an unlimited fine.

She continued: *"It has been a longstanding principle that defendants can rely on their own good character as evidence in their defence. The defendant's good character may be shown by his reputation or indeed by the absence of any previous convictions. Therefore, defendants who do not have previous convictions are free to rely on this in court as evidence of their good character. However, as I have already stated, the final decision on what penalty to impose rests with the court."*

"A defendant has a right of appeal from the Crown Court to the Court of Appeal (Criminal Division) against conviction and sentence."

She then went on to detail the circumstances required for this.

She signed it with a handwritten message, which said:

"I hope this letter helps in some small way. Very best wishes, Patricia Scotland, Baroness Scotland QC."

My sentencing which was rescheduled due to court staffs' industrial action was set for Tuesday, 29th March. We went to our caravan for Easter as we had done the year before. The sea looked gorgeous as we arrived, lapping onto the sand of the private beach. We had a lovely six days. We washed the caravan then relaxed and enjoyed some time together. John had taken some work and I had taken some writing paper. I wrote a letter to Hazel Blears about my job. This was going to be my next battle. Hazel Blears is the MP for Salford, the local authority I had worked for all my working life. She also held a senior position in the government. I knew that she had been involved in implementing the legislation regarding anti-social behaviour and supported ASBOs so I hoped that she would have some understanding of my situation.

We had a lovely time, walking on the beach and staying up late playing cards. On the way home on the Monday evening, we stopped for a meal at a lovely old pub. I had a big juicy steak with au poire sauce. We arrived home quite late, unloaded the car and went to bed. I was glad that we had enjoyed this time together.

The following morning I was due to be sentenced – Tuesday, 29th March. I got up early and sorted the washing, put the washer on, and threw another four wash loads onto the kitchen floor to finish when I came back. Although I had been advised that prison was 'a possibility', I felt after everything that had been said it was remote. The probation officer had stated that to send me to prison would be 'highly inappropriate'. My barrister had said that she did not believe the judge wanted to send me to prison. I went upstairs to say goodbye to my son James, who was still in bed, before leaving for court. I said: "See ya later, I'm going to get sent to prison now." He grunted something back and went back to sleep.

The press were waiting for us outside court. They took photographs as I walked towards the court, their lenses incessantly clicking. When we got inside I felt nervous but I thought: "These journalists will go mad if I get sent to prison." My family went into the public gallery with the reporters. I had to enter the pulpit-like dock, with two guards standing behind me. When my barrister started to sum up, she got a couple of things wrong. She said I carried the air rifle over my shoulder when in fact it was over my arm, pointed downwards. She said I fired the pistol but omitted to say it was not loaded. This concerned me a little. When the judge started to speak, he read from a piece of paper. I thought: "He has already made up his mind, whatever my barrister said would not have made any difference anyway." He stressed the "seriousness" of the charges on which I had been found guilty and mentioned "vigilante action."

He said: "You assumed that these individuals were likely to be the same individuals who had committed the other anti-social activity. You went out and approached boys who were on Delamere Road near to your home. You shouted abuse at these boys, including the use of bad language. You were, as you concede, ranting and raving like a lunatic. These boys denied any involvement in any of the anti-social acts committed against you and there is no evidence whatsoever that would contradict those denials."

He also said: "Both weapons were capable of causing lethal injury. Those weapons, or at least the air pistol, were kept in your house to frighten burglars. You took those weapons from those separate rooms. Before you left the house with them, you fired the air pistol in the house probably twice and a pellet from the gun almost hit your son who was standing on the landing. You knew what you were doing when you went back to get those guns."

He continued: "The courts in dealing with offences such as those of which you have been convicted, discourage two things: First, vigilante action, which is the taking of the law into one's own hands, secondly, the use and discharge of firearms in a public place. The use and discharge of firearms in a public place is a cause of great public concern. Even on a misunderstanding of the facts here, there can be no excuse whatsoever for what you did that night. Even had those *children* been involved in anti-social activity against you, there was never any suggestion that they had ever armed themselves with any weapon and your response, in going out into the road, at night, with guns, was a wholly disproportionate response. The jury rejected your defence, namely that you only had the gun with you, to protect yourself."

His attitude was completely different to at the trial. His job now was to sentence a guilty person. He started talking about cases which had set precedents and quoting the length of prison sentences. I thought: "Keep calm, you can cope. I can manage a few weeks." I was calmed to a degree by the knowledge that the appeal had been submitted meaning his verdict could be proved wrong and the convictions overturned. The judge continued:

"The Court of Appeal, in the guideline case of Avis, have stated that the courts should treat any offence under the Firearms Act, 1968, as serious. In addition, the Court of Appeal have said that, save for minor infringements, offences under the Act will almost always merit terms of custody, even on a guilty plea and even in the case of an offender with no previous record. A conviction such as yours under section 16(a) often meets with a custodial term of considerable length, particularly with a firearm that is loaded and it has been used, as here, to cause fear of violence.

"Your personal mitigation is considerable, in that you are of positively good character, a 48 year old teacher of children with educational difficulties. I have read testimonials to your character. I have also read and carefully considered the pre-sentence report and the psychiatric report of Dr — — of the 20th January, 2005. I accept all that has been said on your behalf by Ms Arshad, in particular that you acted in a very unfortunate manner, the incident came about when a lot of stressful circumstances had come to a head, I accept you acted totally out of character and I accept that up to that point in time you were a perfectly law-abiding citizen, indeed carrying out a very important job, and doing it very well, as a teacher. I accept that there will be very serious implications for you and your family of a custodial sentence upon you, not just during any term of custody, but also for the remainder of your life. I have read and considered the various authorities that have been put before me by Ms Arshad on your behalf, which show that in appropriate circumstances the courts can, and should, impose short sentences of imprisonment in cases for offences under Section 16(a) of the Firearms Act, 1968. I have read the reference from Kathleen Jordan and also a letter from a member of the public asking me to treat you leniently."

"However, notwithstanding all of that mitigation, I am entirely satisfied that the circumstances of the offences of which you have been convicted are, for the reasons I have set out, so serious that only a custodial sentence can be justified. But for the mitigation advanced on your behalf, the sentence I would impose against you for the firearms offence would be measured in years. However, because of that mitigation, I feel able to impose a shorter sentence. Accordingly, I sentence you as follows. On count 1 of the indictment, the offence under section 16(a) of the Firearms Act, I impose a sentence of six months' imprisonment, on count 2 of the indictment, the offence of affray, the sentence is one of one months' imprisonment, to run concurrently with the sentence of six months. You will serve one half of that sentence in prison, after that time the rest of your sentence will be suspended and you will be released. Your release will not bring this sentence to an end. If, after your release, and before the end of the period covered by the sentence, you commit any further offence, you may be ordered to return to custody to serve the balance of the original sentence outstanding at the date of the further offence, as well as being punished for that new offence."

I felt numb. I was more concerned for my family, who were sitting there hearing this, than myself. I thought: "I can cope but they can't cope without me." I was mainly concerned about John, my daughter, and my dad.

I didn't leave the court. I didn't get to speak to my family. I was led down the steps through a door and down to the cells underneath the courts. There were no windows and it was cold down below ground level. Prison guards were wearing navy ribbed jumpers. I was put in a little room and started to text my friends to tell them that I had been given six months. I was just about to press 'send' when a prison officer came in and took the phone from me. I was taken to see Sue Ann and my barrister who explained that as it was less than a year's sentence, I would only have to serve half of my sentence. That would be three months and I might be able to apply for a tag halfway through the sentence, at six weeks. I said: "I can cope as long as they can cope at home." I asked her to tell them that I was OK and that I would carry on being OK as long as they were.

Then I took off my jewellery, a diamond ring that John had bought me and a diamond wishbone ring, made from my mum's rings, and gave them to Sue Ann for Donna. I said: "Tell her to look after them. I don't want to lose them in prison." I thought it might comfort her to have her mum's rings. My barrister told me that we would appeal against the prison sentence on the grounds that it was 'wrong in principle'. I wrote a note to John of instructions to complete the rest of the wash loads and gave it to Sue Ann. I later found out that my family thought I had sent him a romantic declaration of love but were not surprised to discover that it was washing instructions. I was then taken to the main desk in the centre of a corridor that ran between the cells. My things were taken from me and listed on a piece of paper: my handbag and the mobile phone the officer already had. The female officer couldn't turn it off and asked one of the male officers to help. He said: "Thrown it on the floor – that will turn it off". I thought that he was unnecessarily nasty. The female officer started to sort and list the stuff in my handbag but when she saw what a big job it was, the nasty one said: "Seal it in a bag and let them do it when she gets to prison." I didn't know which prison I was going to but that didn't make any difference to me. I didn't know what any of them were like anyway.

We had been the first case in court at 10 a.m.. Luckily I had eaten a piece of toast at home. I was then put into a cell. It was cold with no windows. I sat on a pad on a concrete shelf and looked at the white tiled walls. It was very dimly lit and semi-dark. They brought around a sandwich for lunch at around 1 p.m. but I couldn't eat anything and refused. I had a red hot cup of tea in a plastic cup. You were not allowed pottery, probably because you could break it and self-harm or use it as a weapon. As the day went on, the cells got fuller and noisier. Girls were shouting from the women's side to the men's side. They said things like: "What you in for?" and "Where do you come from?" There were a lot of suggestive comments.

At 4 p.m. a guard came and I was handcuffed to be taken from the cell to the white prison van. The driver told me I had been on the radio and I felt like Myra Hindley or some other infamous criminal. When I got in the van they said I had to sit in a chair cell. There were eight cells on the van, four down each side, each having a locked door. I said: "I can't get in there because I get claustrophobic" and started to get upset. They insisted I went in. I asked if they could leave the door open but they couldn't. They said I could sit at the front and they would put the radio on. There was only me in the van. I had no choice but to get in. The heavy metal door clanged shut and the keys turned in the lock. There was one seat in the cell with no seat belt because you could hang yourself with them. I thought of all the times I had seen these vans on the news for nonorious criminals like Shipman and Fred West.

I watched through the small square window. The colours outside were tainted, all in shades of brown. As we drove through the centre of Manchester it was like watching a scene from a film. I was there, but not in it. I had been removed from society. The van headed out of the city centre, past Piccadilly and towards Stockport. It called at Stockport Magistrates' Court where I had been tried, and picked up two women. They got in and started shouting questions like: "Got any cigs?" and "Wot you in for?" I couldn't be bothered shouting back to them. They carried on shouting to each other and seemed quite unaffected by their environment, quite used to the experience. They were trying to cadge cigarettes from the guard on board.

PART 3

Prison Diaries

20   Strip Searched and Incarcerated

Tuesday, 29th March, 2005

I watched the countryside pass by through the small window as we approached Styal prison. I saw the sign for the prison and we drove up a long drive then entered through a barrier and large metal gates which were about 20ft high. I could see a high metal mesh fence, the front section of which was topped with razor wire. As the van stopped outside the reception house, I could see large old Georgian red brick houses with red tiled roofs and sash windows. I thought: "They could be lovely houses, the kind footballers would have". I then noticed that these had bars over the windows. I thought: "They won't keep me here for long, the appeal application proves the case against me wasn't truthful, someone will do something about this."

I was taken out of the van and into the reception. I didn't have to be handcuffed now as I was in an enclosed prison. The staff seemed warm and welcoming and the reception was clean, bright and sunny. It had a wooden and glass-brick reception desk a bit like a hotel's, but there the resemblance finished. I was asked to sit in a little room separated by a glass partition. A notice on the door read: "Prisoners not strip searched". I was filled with trepidation. It was unnerving not knowing what fate awaited me. I was called out to the desk to give my details, be photographed, and was given a prisoner number – 4108 – and an identity card. I then moved to the next but one room and my personal possessions were examined and listed. My remaining jewellery was to be put in a safe but I was allowed to keep my eternity ring – a present from John – and a pair of earrings. The contents of my handbag took a while to sort through. I had items for every eventuality and it hit me that I didn't need them now. I snapped up my credit cards and put them in the bin. I emptied my purse, which contained £47.50. This was put into my private prisoner account. The clothes I was wearing were logged. I was to wear these for six days.

I was then called into a cubicle. It was like a public toilet with melamine panels and inside were two prison officers wearing rubber gloves. The door was locked and they explained that every prisoner had to be strip searched. I was told to remove all my clothing below the waist, which was inspected and then given back to me. I then had to remove all my clothing above the waist which was also inspected. It was a very degrading experience, a ritual that signified that I was now a prisoner and as such not entitled to any dignity. A woman then made me a cup of tea and explained that I would spend two nights in the 'first night house' and that it was 'very nice'. It had only been open for two weeks and had cost £270,000 to refurbish. I thought that the people I was talking to were staff but they were in fact inmates, whose job it was to work on reception. I was told that I would then be moved onto a 'house' and that they were very nice.

The first night house is a new facility introduced to cut down on the stress to new prisoners coming in to prison. It has a nice lounge with cream tie-back drapes, a wide-screen TV and leather sofas. Previously I would have been put straight onto Waite wing. I am grateful for the benefit of this facility. I sat in front of the TV and read the paper. My story is all over the papers and on the TV news. I am very grateful for all the support the media are giving me. I still feel nervous though about what is going to happen to me. I have been told the first night house was a measure introduced to reduce the incidence of suicide at this prison. Apparently there were six suicides in the year from 2002 to 2003 and someone has told me that that there were 47 suicide attempts by women in this prison on Mother's Day two weeks earlier. What a sad tale of woe!

I feel like I should be strong because I have a loving family. A lot of the women here have had their children taken off them. I feel comforted by the love of John and my children. I have been allowed a £2 phone credit from my money and phoned home to tell them I am ok and how 'lovely' it is in here. I told them I have an en-suite room (although actually it's just a sink and loo) and that I will be ok as long as they are which is true. Staff 'on the house' (as it is referred to here) are very considerate and the other prisoners are polite and pleasant. Some work on the house as their 'job', housekeeping or as 'listeners' who are people who you can talk to and ask for advice about prison life and routine. Most of the inmates are young. One girl seemed very stressed and upset. We can have a free tobacco pack so I took it and gave it to her as I don't smoke. She later told me that she had stabbed and killed her husband. Although this was shocking I felt sorry for her as I got the impression she had been subject to years of abuse. I felt privileged again to have the security of a loving family.

Wednesday, 30th March

On my first full day in prison a succession of people came to see me and interview me for various purposes including a nurse, who is also a psychiatric nurse, the chaplain, and two women from the probation service who told me they can contact my solicitor on my behalf. They are very cheerful, I suppose that is part of their job. I also got the general induction to prison life from the officers.

In prison, lunch is at 12 noon and tea is at 5 p.m. I have decided that while I am in prison, I might as well try to lose some weight. I am going to go to the gym to improve my fitness. Then at least my time in here will not have been wasted. The food is not very good but I try to eat the healthy part of it and leave the stodge. We are given a breakfast pack at lunch for the next day including four tea bags and sachets of sugar a single cereal pack, jam for toast and a small carton of UHT milk. They are all unlabelled makes and the prison bread tastes like sawdust. Lunch isn't much better. You get a barmcake – mine had rubbery cheese and a piece of fruit. I got a hard little pear which would be better used as ammunition. It would be more effective than my air pistol!

In the evening the inmates from the first night house were taken on a tour of the prison. Unfortunately it was raining. I was relieved because I had been told I was definitely going into a 'house' and not onto the Wing. We looked at the houses, about 14 of them. One was a mother and baby unit for prisoners who are pregnant when they are jailed. The buildings are separated by grassed lawned areas linked by tarmac drives with flagged paths to the houses but the whole place has an eerie atmosphere dominated by the presence of 'The Wing'. It is a grey, metal building with a corrugated roof and is surrounded by a high security rolled razor wire topped fence. It is a prison within a prison. The outer high metal mesh fence that surrounds the prison can always be seen wherever you are, like a reminder. As I walked around, other prisoners shouted at me from the houses recognising me from all the publicity. One voice, shouting: "Linda, you should have fucking bazookered em!"

When we got back I was told when I leave the first night house tomorrow I will go onto the Wing! Waite Wing is where prisoners who are on drugs and are de-toxing are put, as well as self-harmers and those who are not deemed to have sufficient social skills to cope with the independence of being on a house. I protested and said I had been told I was being put on a house but I was told that that was wrong, because of the serious and violent nature of my crime and the fact it was a firearms offence, meant I had to be put on the Wing! My sense of doom and trepidation returned.

Thursday, 31st March

This morning I was told that I can now definitely go onto a house because the governor has apparently given 'special permission' subject to my background checks being clear. I must not have been arrested, warned or even cautioned for anything whatsoever or I would not be able to go on a house.

My family came to see me this afternoon. I gave a statement to Donna to read to the press which I had written on prison paper. It passed my thanks on to our neighbours and strangers for their support. It also said

"We have applied to appeal against the conviction on the grounds of 'new evidence' which proves that what I was telling the police was correct.

I shot an unloaded air pistol at the pavement when I was threatened by a convicted criminal."

The statement was initially taken off me by a prison officer. Apparently I am not allowed to pass things to visitors. She later came over and told us my daughter could collect it on her way out.

John, Donna, James and my dad came on the visit. It was lovely to see them. I held and kissed them all in turn. When I held Donna I could feel the pain as she held me tight and started to tremble. I felt the same way. Being segregated and isolated from my family is the worst thing. I do not know how people cope who do not have the support of their family or are sent miles away from home. They brought me some clothes but they have been sent to reception until I am allowed to collect them. I am desperate to change my clothes. The visit was spent discussing all the practicalities of how they are going to cope at home. What's in the freezer, sorting out our interconnected finances etc. I normally sort everything like that out. The visit went really quickly and soon it was time for them to go. I hoped they'd feel better now that they had seen me, as I did after seeing them. James, who is not demonstrative of his feelings at all, stared back at me as he queued to leave the visiting hall. His gaze did not leave me and he waved as he left the room.

As I returned to the house in the sunshine, I didn't feel so isolated. When I got back I had to put my possessions in a plastic sack to take over to 'Barker House', my new home. When I arrived there, the inmates were mostly sitting in the common room watching television. They seem a friendly bunch. They all said: "We know who you are, and what you're in for". They had all seen me on the television. I was taken into the office to be told which shared bedrooms had a vacancy and who they were with. I chose to share with Carol, who is my age and not in for anything violent. She is in for fraud, having embezzled £2 million from Norwich Union. Maria the housekeeper, on the first night house, had already told me that she was a very nice woman. She only arrived last week herself. I unpacked my belongings and called home to tell them where I am. They told me that reporters from Granada TV had knocked on the door and they had read the statement to them, and to make sure I watched "Granada Reports" tonight. I saw Donna on the telly reading the statement. She looked lovely and all the girls said how gorgeous she was and I felt very proud. John came across as the very nice and genuine person he is. James kept out of the way of the publicity as usual. Craig thinks the publicity is great. It's so funny how different they are.

The house is locked up at 8.30 p.m. The common room is locked but we have televisions in our rooms and can wander down to use the pay phone any time as long as we have the credit. The phone lines go dead around midnight for twenty minutes because all phone calls are recorded and this is when they change the tapes. Carol and I choose our viewing for the evening. It is 'Footballers' Wives' followed by a film. I am looking forward to phoning home before going to bed. The mattresses are narrow and hard and no more than one inch thick. I can feel the metal strips of the bed through the mattress and notice how horrible it smells, very stale and unpleasant. I think I will need to be very tired to sleep on this.

21   Porridge in Barker House

Friday, 1st April

All the girls in the house who go to education classes stayed on the house today as it is still the Easter holidays. Some of the girls went out to work – in the stores or the garden – but the house was still very busy. I got myself organised putting 'apps' in, applications for things I want to sort out. I put in an application to get my hair done at a training salon in the education department. I've also put my name down for a gym induction on Sunday morning and asked the officer to complete a PVO – Privileged Visiting Order – for me. Only two visits per month are allowed for up to three adults but a PVO is an extra visit given one a month for good behaviour. It will be sent out to my family and they will arrange a convenient time and book the appointment by phone.

I mopped out my room with some strong pine disinfectant to try to get rid of the nasty smell. It has worked for now. I spent the afternoon writing to people and answering the many cards and letters I have received from well-wishers all over the country. A man from London has written and even offered to pay my legal expenses! There are so many caring people out there that I know I will not have time to answer them all. So instead I decided to write a standard letter which can be copied, put all the addresses on envelopes, and send them out to Donna to post for me. This created a problem because I did not have enough envelopes. The girls on the house have been very kind and three of them gave me their envelopes until I could get some sent in. I've also started to get letters and cards from old colleagues and friends who I haven't seen for years and who have heard about my predicament in the media.

I spoke to Donna tonight and she had some surprising news. Apparently the investigating DS has been getting hate mail and has also been stalked. She was quite excited by this. He was apparently accosted at a petrol station but I don't know where she has heard this from. Maybe it's been in the paper. People must recognise him because he has been on the television so much trying to justify why he charged me. Apparently, outside the court, he was interviewed about the sentence and had said: "It was just." It would seem that people disagree.

One younger officer who is pregnant said she had thought of me when she got very annoyed at some little children who had picked her daffodils and thrown them on the road. She said if they had wanted to take them home for their mums, she wouldn't have been so upset. It is very upsetting when people damage your property on purpose for no reason.

Saturday, 2nd April

On Saturday we are all allocated jobs to share the weekend housework. I was on the list for watering the plants in the house. There are loads of plants in the house, in the common room, dining room, utility room, on the landing, in the bathroom, shower room and both toilets. It reminds me of being at home, pottering around watering plants. I thought: "If this is the worst they can do to me, I can stand this until someone gets me out."

I phoned home, John seemed quite bright. He says the phone is ringing all the time with friends offering support and the press are constantly at the door. Donna and Rob are also busy setting up a Free Linda website and my friends 'the girls' are setting up a 'Justice for Linda Walker campaign'! They're getting t-shirts printed and setting up a petition starting on Wednesday in Manchester. The Manchester Evening News are also involved apparently so it all sounds promising. This is all very heartening to me, even quite exciting. The girls on the house have awarded me 'celebrity status'. This was quite a good day. I continued to try to choose the healthy options on offer at meal times and have fruit where possible. One of the girls, Dawn, started a daft game of 'hide and seek' after tea so I joined in and shouted "Coming, ready or not" and went to seek her out. We had a laugh and it broke the boredom. John has apparently reported to the press that I am "in good spirits" and the prison is reported as saying that I am "settling in".

Sunday, 3rd April

At 8.30 a.m. I went for my gym induction and got issued with a pass. The publicity is full on now and I read about myself in the Sunday papers. The Daily Mail had written a two page spread which was very sympathetic. I phoned home and John was busy getting a roast in the oven as his daughter Rachel was coming for tea it was her birthday yesterday. I can only phone certain people whose numbers I have nominated and these are home, Donna, Craig, dad and James' mobile for an emergency as it was the only mobile number which I could remember. If

I do not buy any treats with the weekly money allowed, which are ordered via a sheet referred to as 'canteen', I can have all my 'wages' on phone credit and this will be up to £16. As I have not been able to work yet, I was only given a £3.50 allowance for this week. The phone is quite expensive, I believe it's 9p per minute, which seems to swallow up the credit, but I feel at the moment I need to keep in contact as much as possible for my own sake as well as theirs.

Monday, 4th April

Everyone who 'works' was out of the house today except for Carol and I, who don't yet have 'jobs', and Ellen, who does the housekeeping as her job, was also around. Ellen is a very nice lady, who is a few years older than me. She told me the judge told her: "I think the best thing I can do for you Mrs H is to separate you from alcohol and alcohol from you! Six months." Then he banged his hammer and she said: "Thank you, your honour." She makes me laugh. After lunch I got sent to the education department, where I did a basic numeracy and literacy test. I was a bit disgusted with myself because I got two spellings and four maths questions wrong! I was then interviewed to establish what I wanted to do regarding education classes or a job. I said I would like to do basic IT as I'm so hopeless that people always do it for me rather than showing me how to do it so I have never learned how to use a computer. I also volunteered to help with literacy in the afternoon. This took up the afternoon for me and after tea I went to the gym and started using the cycling and rowing machines. I then returned to the house. It was a good night on television and I did not want to miss Coronation Street.

I rang home and Donna told me that PW 1 had been

appealing for my release! She said it was front page headlines in the Manchester Evening News, "Release Her Now!" He had apparently told reporter Yakub Queshi "I can understand why she did it. She had some reason for it and I hoped she would have just got a warning." I said I knew he wasn't all bad and don't think he ever intended that I would go to prison. John told me that the press were still as manic and the only way he could get rid of them was to talk to them. He said he had been interviewed by Granada in the back garden. He apologised for talking to Eleanor Moritz from the BBC on the front drive. He knew I was unhappy with her reporting at the time of the trial. I thought that this may have had a negative influence on public opinion and maybe even the jury, I watched the news though anyway and it was nice to see John and our home and garden.

22   Settling in and Making Friends

Tuesday, 5th April

I have been in custody for a week today and it is a damn sight easier than going to work. It was a normal day in what was now becoming my routine. I am getting to know the prison officers who are very considerate and kind toward me, I treat them respectfully accepting the role of prisoner and their authority as an officer, it is easiest.

I did not realise I would start my IT class so soon so I did not go out at 9 a.m. when education was called, however at 9.45 a.m. I was sent for. 'Movement' had by that time ceased – you are only allowed to move around between certain times of day – and the houses were locked so I needed a movement pass to walk the 200 yards to the house where the education department is situated. While in the class I mix with some of the women from the wing. They are different from the women on the houses. Most come to classes late as they have to go for 'meds' – their medication. Usually it is methadone as many of them are addicted to heroin. They speak about other prisoners' crimes such as arson and someone going to be sentenced for attempting to kill the same person three times and such like.

They speak of prisoners 'cutting up bad' on the wing, which is a reference to the many seriously disturbed people who self-harm. They have been put in prison because there is nowhere more appropriate for them to go. Really, they should be in hospital. The prevalence of mental illness is very high. A lot of these people need help but it would seem that prison is now the only option to keep them safe and get them the support they require.

I went to the gym again tonight and stayed a bit longer but I am not really enthralled by it. I am finding out now why I have never really bothered with exercise when I was free. When I phoned home, John seemed upset. He said he has forgotten to get the ham, which James has on his butties every day. John has been making them for him and ironing his shirts for work. Prior to me coming to prison James had joked: "When you go to prison mum, who's going to make my butties?" This wound John up. He didn't like the idea of me going to prison or appreciate the joke that his only worry was that I wouldn't be there to make his butties. All that was forgotten now as John worried that he had forgotten the ham. I told him that there were tins of ham in the shed but he said James had told him he didn't like tinned ham. I told him a secret. If you scrape the jelly off and cut the ham really thin, he doesn't know the difference. I wondered if John had done this. Probably not, knowing John.

Wednesday, 6th April

I heard today from John that there is a bail hearing for my appeal next Wednesday. He said my dad is sorting out £5,000 to put up for surety. Staff keep telling me I will probably get out on bail soon with all the fuss in the papers. So I could be out this time next week. I am buzzing. I have IT class this morning and this afternoon I have a visit. Donna, my brother Chris, and Craig are coming. On the television in the lunch time news, the police were complaining about receiving hate mail because of my case. They said they were going to investigate but apparently there is too much. Sackfuls! This has really cheered me up. Thank you British public! The police however are complaining that they are 'misinformed'!!

I got ready for my visit. I washed my hair and borrowed some mascara so I didn't look too haggard. I had a lovely visit. Donna was full of the website and the support we are getting. They are relieved that I got put on a house. I am having my hair done tomorrow in the training salon and hopefully I should be home next week. John was on the television at tea time. The phone-in polls on television and in the papers are coming out at 96 to 98 per cent public opinion that I should not be in prison. I am receiving around 20 cards and letters a day from all over the country. A lot of them are from eminent people such as a professor, magistrate, serving and ex-police officers and titled people. I have had a lot from older people who are frightened to go out because of yobs, and other victim families living in terror. There are many harrowing tales. One old person sent me £20 and told me to buy myself a box of chocolates! This got put into my private money before it got to me. I am trying to answer all my mail, even if only with the standard letter.

Carol and I got the new mattresses today the old smelly ones have been taken away. They are still only two inches thick, hard and compact and I can still feel the bars of the two feet wide bed, but at least they don't stink. Two of the girls in our house work in the stores so we got them first when they came in.

Thursday, 7th April

I had an appointment today to get my hair done. One of the hairdressing students, Nadine, is in our house and she got me in. She is a nice girl, every now and again when she gets bored she gives us a 'Whitney Houston' concert in the common room. She is funny and has a very good voice. She even looks a little bit like Whitney. I had my roots coloured and a full head tint, this took all morning and there was no time for my cut so I had to go back in the afternoon for it. This meant I had to miss my class, helping as an orderly with literacy, so I had a very nice day today. At least my hair will look decent for when I get released next Wednesday!!

Friday, 8th April

I had a legal visit from Sue Ann today, to tell me about the bail hearing and the appeal. When she came, she had loads to tell me and seemed worried she might run out of time so she ended up telling me in a big rush. I kept chipping in which didn't help because then she lost her flow. She and my barrister think I will get bail but they don't want to promise me this. She confirmed my dad has offered to pay a £5,000 surety. I am worried that if I don't do the sentence and the conviction isn't overturned, I will have to return to prison later to complete the sentence. I would rather finish it now if that were to be the case. Also, I am worried that if the sentence is reduced, I may get a fine or costs instead and end up loosing our home. As it stands now I still have my home and I have been informed I could be out with an electronic tag on a Home Detention Curfew on the thirteenth of May. Sue Ann informed me that the appeal against sentence has already gone in and that the risk of all this is unlikely. She suggested that possibly I could sell my story to the papers to pay any costs incurred if there are any. She said press interest at the office is manic. She showed me a statement that they wanted to release on my behalf to satisfy the press' curiosity and I agreed to the statement. Despite my concerns about the appeal, I decided I would go along with whatever my legal advisors thought was best.

Everything seems to have gone quiet in the papers and on television as the news is dominated by the Pope and his funeral and on Saturday, the Royal Wedding. I have been joking around the house that I am going to watch it in a posh hat.

Saturday, 9th April

I did watch the Royal Wedding on television, which shows how bored I am. The girls on the house were more interested in the Grand National and had a sweep stake, the winner to be bought a treat from canteen by everyone. At night I pretended to be a ghost with sheets over my head, coming up the stairs and made the girls scream and laugh. The mood in the house is quite light hearted. I am feeling quite relaxed and thinking about going home, but am bored. I have told John that I am bored but he is so busy he has not got any time to be bored. I do not have a lot of credit a left for the phone, I could only put £3 onto the phone (whole pounds only) with only getting the basic £3.50 allowance this week.

Sunday 10th April

I am getting more bored now as there is nothing to do on the house except to watch television read and answer my letters and none arrive on a Sunday. I keep thinking of all the jobs

I could be getting done at home but this hopefully is my last weekend here, which is a comforting thought. I have used nearly all my phone credit and have only got twenty pence left. I have told John to sort out paying my bail tomorrow and he said: "I will try". I said: "What do you mean, you'll try?" He then said: "I will."

Monday, 11th April

I went to education, IT class this morning. I am realising why I have always avoided computers like the plague, they are very boring, especially so for me because I am so slow and have to keep waiting for the teacher to show me how to do things. Then I forget straightaway and I have to ask the same thing again a few minutes later. Then they don't do what they should, even the teacher has to fiddle with the stupid machine to get it to do what I want. In the afternoon I helped a girl to complete some literacy work booklets. She completed five of them which is the whole week's work in one afternoon. The teacher was very pleased. The girl, who was only about nineteen, told me she is in for offences related to heroin, she looked a bit like a zombie with emptiness in her eyes. She told me that her baby was taken off her, and a friend had said if she took heroin it would help her get rid of the pain. She said it did but then she got put in prison. Also she was pregnant when she came into prison but lost the baby due to coming straight off the heroin. She said the prison had not sorted out her methadone – replacement for the heroin – soon enough so she lost the baby. I felt very sorry for her and realised why her eyes looked so empty. As we worked through the worksheets, they were so boring we both agreed you could die of terminal boredom in here.

When I got back to the house I was half expecting to hear

about my bail, that the £5,000 has been paid and I could go, (forgetting that the hearing is not until Wednesday). But I didn't hear anything. John is at work until 9 p.m. on Monday doing an evening class, so I can't contact him till later. I tried his number at work but I couldn't get through as the phone number is not one of my approved numbers. I have kept my approved numbers to relatives only, as I do not get enough phone credits to phone friends as well and I can always get John to pass messages to friends. I have found out that 'the girls,' my friends, were outside the prison yesterday, from girls who saw the lunchtime news, demonstrating for my release. I found this very comforting. They came on the 6.00 p.m. news and I proudly told everyone who each one is. Then I busied myself reading and sorting my letters.

When I got through to John I asked him: "Why am I still here?" He said Sue Ann was off sick so he left a message for the solicitor to ring him but she hasn't phoned back. I asked: "Well why didn't you ring again or why didn't you ask for someone else, Adam knows about things."

Adam also works at the office. John said he didn't know, so I asked: "Why didn't you go down? It is only on Princess Parkway." He said he didn't know where it was. I said: "You do, you've been. I rang at eight this morning and you were out, you don't need to go to work until twelve noon, why did you not sort my bail first? Do you not want me to be released? Am I not your priority?" He said: "Yes of course you are," but he didn't seem to have done much about it, then my phone credit ran out so I was stranded. Credit does not go on now until Wednesday evening, I haven't got a clue what's going on and I can't find out. It sounded like nothing was being done about getting me out anyway, I felt forgotten and deserted. Luckily I had put an application in to see the probation officer. I know

John will be really upset at home now as if I am upset it always upsets John, and now I can't even talk to him.

Tuesday, 12th April

The probation officer came to see me today. I am getting really stressed now. I explained that I thought I would have bail by now and that I needed to speak to my solicitor. I told her I could not phone as I have no credit. She telephoned for me, the house officer let us use her office for the call, when I got to speak to her I could hardly speak because I was too upset. I said: "Why hasn't John sorted my bail and why aren't I out of here? I thought I was getting bail." She explained I have misunderstood, that the bail is not just a matter of paying over the money but has to be approved by the judge at the bail hearing on Wednesday. She said she had spoken to John and had arranged to phone him every day at 5 p.m. to tell him what was happening, so he could tell me when I rang. She said my barrister was going to London on Wednesday for the bail hearing. I told this to the probation officer who said she would arrange for me to have some more phone credit put on from my private money, the money I had brought in with me, so that I could ring John and find out what was happening.

I rang John at 6 p.m. and told him I had got some phone credit put on and that I had got the wrong end of the stick about the bail but should be home tomorrow after the hearing. John said Craig was there and asked if I wanted to speak to him. I did, and he asked: "Shall I make a buffet for when you get home tomorrow?" I said: "Don't be daft, wait till I am home first." I didn't want to tempt fate, so I went off on a cheery note. I went to my room and packed my plastic sack ready for going home in the morning, I wanted to make sure I was ready and didn't need to stay here a moment a longer than necessary. I felt sorry for Carol as she was in the room whilst I was packing. She had only come in the week before me so she was still trying to accustom herself to the two and a half years she has to do, whilst I am hopefully on my way home.

23   Bail Decision

Wednesday, 13th April

When I woke up, I thought: "This is the day I get released." I could hardly wait, I know the solicitor had said she "couldn't promise" but she was just being overcautious, I thought. They could not, not let me out – 98% of the British public think I should not be in prison. I went to my I. T. class, I thought of asking to stay on the house to be near the phone, but then I thought I could be there all day, best to keep busy. I was only in the class for an hour and an officer came in to get me, I thought: "This is it I am on my way." The officer said I was to return to the house. As I walked back in the spring sunshine I thought what should I do if I haven't got my release on bail? But then I thought the worst thing that could happen is that I would have to stay here a bit longer.

I went into the office on the house, two officers were there, they shut the door, they seemed apprehensive, they said: "Bad news Linda, you haven't got it." I felt totally deflated, I couldn't believe why anyone would want to keep me here, I also felt angry. So I said: "I'm on hunger strike, I've had no breakfast and I'm not going to have anything else except water." The prison officers then tried to talk me out of that, saying: "Stay strong for your fight," and: "Stay strong for your family," but I was having none of it. I didn't want to eat, I wasn't hungry. The food was shit anyway and I was too distressed to eat. I had already told my family if I did not get out I would hunger strike anyway so it would be no shock to them. I had gone on hunger strike when I got arrested, it was a protest against injustice.

I asked about getting a tag, I thought if I couldn't get out on bail pending my appeal, at least a tag, HDC (home detention curfew) when you have to be home for 7 p.m., would mean I could be home for my boys' 18th birthdays on the 18th May. The date for my HDC eligibility was the 13th May and even though I would miss John's birthday, on 30th April and the bank holiday weekend (Mayday) I thought at least I would be at home with my family for the boys' birthday and the Whit Week holiday. The officers seemed hesitant about a tag. They said that because of the offence they didn't think I could have a tag, because it was 'firearms'. The custody lady was down by this point and she said she would find out for me. They were all very concerned for me but it was getting worse, my options were all having the doors slammed shut on them.

I did not go to education in the afternoon I stayed on the house to write a letter to the judge who is to hear my appeal. The officers didn't ask me to go, I wrote my letter but wanted to type it up, so I asked Miss Hardwick if I could be allowed to use the computer in my I. T. class and she said "yes," even though it is not allowed to do private work in the class really.

I phoned John when he got home. He said he doesn't think I will win the appeal. He thinks they have got it in for me. The police want to look like they are getting tough on firearms offences – but I didn't think that what I did could really be classed as a dangerous firearms incident. The police had contacted John to have a meeting about his police complaint but had then cancelled because they were having a meeting about me! I asked John if he had told the press about my hunger strike. He said he hadn't so I said: "So I've starved since last night to make a protest and no one even knows?" He said "OK, I'll sort it." I went off the phone and went into the common room. A few minutes later a breaking news text came across the bottom of the television screen – Linda Walker on hunger strike. I was really surprised and quite amazed at the power I had to influence the news. It was on the news later also.

Thursday, 14th April

Still on hunger strike, I have only had water and no food since Tuesday tea time. I feel dizzy and have a headache but I am not a bit hungry. I went to my IT class and started to type up my letter. The teacher John worried about me doing private work in class phoned Miss Hardwick, our house officer, to check I have permission and to his surprise it was confirmed. After an hour I was called back to the house, a Senior Officer tried to talk me out of being on hunger strike but again I refused. I was told I would have to be put on a 20/52 which is like a suicide watch, as it is a form of self harm. I was also put on an ACP (activated care plan) and a file was opened on me. At lunch time I received a letter from the custody officer saying that HDC (home detention curfew) was not available to prisoners with firearms convictions but may be allowed in exceptional circumstances and inviting me to write to the governor if I think this applies to me.

At 2 p.m. I had a legal visit from Sue Ann. She hadn't been to London the day before as I had thought. She said the legal aid only paid for the barrister to go to London. She apologised for being off on Monday but said she was really poorly. I knew she would not be off unless she was as she is very conscientious. She offered to get me a drink and a bar of chocolate from the vending machine but I told her: "I can't because I'm on hunger strike." She brought in the bail notice for me to see but I had already received it. Miss Tiplady the Senior Officer, telephoned the court and got it faxed through for me yesterday. It said: "Bail refused", with reasons and a signature written by the Hon Mr Justice Royce.

"Offences such as these almost invariably attract a custodial sentence often of greater length than six months. The fresh evidence may be of more relevance to sentence than to conviction. The applications have a relatively early listing – provisionally 5th May – before the Vice President. Bail is not justified in these circumstances."

Sue Ann told me the date was a mistake and it was now going to be the 4th of May, the day before the general election. She thinks they are going to reduce my sentence. As I will have already done five weeks and two days – three days off the equivalent of a three month sentence – they will probably released me as that is half my sentence. I am not so confident any longer. I think there is a hidden agenda. I also think it most odd that my appeal is on the 4th of May, the day before the General Election.

My case has been made very political. The issues which it raises are very high profile: Antisocial behaviour, Householder's right to protect home, property and family, Ineffective policing and the fairness of the courts and justice system. Many MPs have raised my case on the television and in the papers. The leader of the conservative party Michael Howard has been using it as evidence of the breakdown of law and order in Britain, against the government. I thought that was rich coming

163

from him when it was his party who systematically dismantled British industry and got rid of all the good jobs traditionally done by working class males – the ones incidentally who are now 'yobs!'

I do not accept that the new evidence: "may be of more relevance to sentence than conviction." The new evidence proves the main police witness lied under oath. If we could have presented the new evidence of the milkman at trial, we could have proved that the main witness for the prosecution was actually lying in the evidence he was giving against me in court. This may have influenced the jury never mind the sentence, there may then have been no sentence to reduce. I made this point to Sue Ann and she agreed. I told her I did not know if I wanted to go to the appeal because I would have to travel to Holloway prison in London and I did not want to be left in Holloway if we lost, rotting until the 29th of June. I needed to apply for HDC because if I get it I will then be due for release on the 13th of May. This being the case, I could go to London for the appeal, safe in the knowledge of only having nine days left of my sentence. If not I think I would rather stay here and wait to hear. Sue Ann told me that she and my barrister were coming to see me next Thursday to prepare for the appeal. That is their plan anyway.

I then return to the house to draft my letter to the governor to apply for a HDC. I know exactly what I want to say, I don't know if it is the 'politically correct' thing to say, but then it was my mouth that got me into trouble in the first place so I thought: "I might as well go the whole hog and at least have the satisfaction of saying what I think."

I wrote: "My boys, unbeknown to me, were suffering a bullying campaign. I stepped out of line once and the police and judiciary came down on me like a ton of bricks – for their own purposes of securing a political charge. As a teacher I have supported people all my life, as a teacher of special needs students and pupils, but when I needed a bit of support from the establishment, no-one was there for me." I included a copy of a letter from my MP, Bev Hughes, which she had sent to me in prison. In it, she said that she was "very sorry" to hear about the outcome of the trial.

She added: "John gave me a full account of the trial itself, which made the jury's final verdict all the more surprising. As you know, I had already taken up various concerns with Greater Manchester Police and the Crown Prosecution Service. I've now written to the Attorney General and enclosed copies of those letters." I thought this would demonstrate the 'exceptional circumstances' of my case. It must surely be unusual for prisoners to get letters such as that from their MP?

On the house after the officer leaves and locks the door at 8.30 p.m., security staff come round at 9.30 p.m. and 6.30 p.m. to count or 'roll check' that all prisoners are there. They are usually ladies and very nice. They will know all about my hunger strike as I am on a 20/52. I have not thought a lot about it, being too busy writing letters but when you are on 'suicide watch', they don't just count you. They check you for movement. They shine their torch in your face to check that you are still breathing. Anyway, they sat and watched Footballers' Wives with us tonight, for a good 20 minutes. They said the whole prison was watching and they didn't want to miss it (it was the DNA testing of the babies), but I got the feeling they were really staying to check up on me, in a caring sort of way.

24   Hunger Strike and Drug Testing

Friday, 15th April

This morning I was not woken up at the crack of dawn as I was yesterday but I did hear the security guard next to me. Vicki our new pad mate told me later, she was stroking my hair or moving it off my face at least. Vicki thought it was very caring the way she checked me so gently, showing compassion far beyond her duty. I have found all the staff to be caring and compassionate. They have been very supportive to me, at least at the ranks that I have come into contact with. I realise now that my first week was OK because I thought I was going, I didn't think I would have to repeat the same futile routine for very long. To think that you are going and then you don't is very disconcerting. In fact it is downright cruel. My head is aching badly now, when I get out of bed I go dizzy and nearly fall over. What have I ever done to deserve this? Why would anyone want to separate me from my family or put us through this hell?

The mood on the house seems different now I think I am having an unsettling and depressing effect on other people. I heard Dawn getting upset and shouting something about people on hunger strike and how sick of it she is on this house.

This made me feel guilty that I am now upsetting other people, who do not deserve to be upset and have their time made worse by me being miserable. I do not feel hungry although I am aware I am getting weaker, feel dizzy and have a persistent headache; my stomach feels like it is eating itself. John has told me that my son James is on hunger strike at home now, if I am so is he, so I can not keep it up much longer now as he is like a rake anyway and he obviously must be upset about it. But as I don't feel like eating the slop they serve up I may as well stay on it a bit longer. I did collect my 'canteen' yesterday: a bottle of Vimto, a packet of crackers and a box of cheese triangles so I have got something nice to eat when I do come off this hunger strike. They said they would credit the money back to my account if I didn't want the food but I have kept it in the sealed bag in our room. I am drinking plenty of water and thinking of it as a 'detox' I have not eaten now since Tuesday.

I went to my morning IT class but after an hour I was called back to the house by the officer. When I got back, there were two senior officers who wanted to talk to me about the hunger strike. They tried to talk me out of it again, I told them I was going to come off it but not yet. They wanted to know why, so I told them I did not want to look foolish by threatening I would do it and then I didn't. They said that would not be the case. I also told them it was very easy to hunger strike there as the food was awful, I didn't want to eat it. Governor Green arrived. She was one of the junior governors newly promoted I believe and she asked me if I was depressed, which I was not. She asked was there anything, if I didn't like the food, which they could get for me from the kitchen. I said I had been fancying an egg, a boiled egg, but I could not eat one on my own as I know all the girls would like an egg for breakfast. She rang the kitchen to request this. I said not today, I would have it tomorrow. She also requested other food for me; fruit, crackers, triangles, coffee, hot chocolate and extra milk. I had to go over to 'health care' for a check. I thought I would get weighed and have my blood pressure taken but when I see the doctor he asked: "Why have you come?" I said: "I have been sent because I am on hunger strike." He said "OK" and wrote it in my record. I was looked at by the nurse. She weighed me and I was 88 kilo and I was disappointed that I had only lost 2 kilo (4lb) since I came into custody 18 days ago. I was then interviewed by three staff including the very nice young lady Senior Officer (SO) who is pregnant. She is the one who sympathized with me over having her daffodils pinched. They had to complete the ACP booklet because of my hunger strike.

I returned to Barker House but it was too late to go back to my IT class so I watched the television and read the paper. There was a small article on my hunger strike in the Daily Express. After lunch we were told not to go back to work as we were having a voluntary drugs test. Barker House is a VTU (voluntary drug-testing unit) which means we co-operate with being tested for drugs at any time, although Mandatory Drug Tests are also given. The prison has targets to reach relating to clear drug tests. The testing unit is in the ground floor of one of the houses, the one nearest to the wing. We all sat together, the girls from Barker House, waiting to go in one by one. The girls with visits this afternoon went in first, followed by the ones who wanted to wee the most. I was not bothered about going in. I waited because I was not particularly keen to return to the class where I support students with their literacy. When I did go in, it involved having a wee in front of a nurse and an officer into a small plastic pot, keeping your hands where you can be seen. They do not look directly at you but it is their job to ensure the test is reliable. I did not find it offensive as some people do, it is the price we pay to stay on the VTU, which means I am with the people who are off drugs and not with the other prisoners who are drug addicts and as such unpredictable. The staff are just following procedures.

I turned down the certificate showing I was drug free although some people collect them. They help them to get probation or towards getting their children back. Apparently last week one house was mandatory drugs tested and four people showed positive for heroin. The one who had a visit the day previously was in trouble, on report and probably back on the wing by now with no visits. Drugs do get into this prison. A woman works patrolling with two dogs full time. One is a chocolate Labrador the other a golden spaniel and they are always in the visiting hall. When they are brought into the house, class or whatever, which they periodically are, you have to stand still while you are sniffed. If the dog sits down next to you he has smelled drugs and you are in trouble. This prison is full of drug addicts. Many treat it as a 'Betty Ford Clinic', coming here to get off drugs and get fit and well. Chrissie on the house says she has put on four stone since coming into prison. She was a heroin addict. There are many people in prison whose lives have been ruined by drugs.

A lot of women are also in prison because of men. I read in a newspaper produced for prisoners about a young woman, also in Styal, who had reported her partner for physically abusing her children to the school which they attended. She was frightened of him and thought they would help her. She was now in prison for failing to protect them. Whilst seemingly in direct conflict a Polish woman was in custody for killing her husband. He was sexually abusing their thirteen year old daughter and when he would not stop she had stabbed him once with a knife. Unfortunately for her he died. She seemed a lovely woman and had a very loving family.

When I returned to the house it was not worth returning to education as it was 3.15 p.m. and classes finish at 4 p.m. I was called into the office again to be told that John had phoned and he was upset. He was supposed to be visiting tomorrow but had rang for an appointment and they were all full and Sunday as well. Monday there are no visits so he can't come until Tuesday. He had left booking until 24 hours before, because he misread the Visiting Order which read: "Valid for 28 days, booking up to 24 hours before". He had taken this to mean he could not book until 24 hours before the visit. He was worried I would be upset and not come off the hunger strike. It did not make a lot of difference to me although I was looking forward to it. I could now look forward to it until Tuesday.

When I rang home in the evening John was very apologetic. He also had bad news about my job. He told me they are having a hearing about me at the local education authority in Salford on 19th April and want any information regarding the charge of gross misconduct against me five days prior to this date – that was yesterday! He had rang them and has also spoken to my union representative who is going to ask for the meeting to be postponed. I told him to post me the papers so I can read everything. He said there is a report on my case from the police, he said: "They really have it in for you Linda, it is awful." Now we know what their meeting was about the other day. I told him: "Send it in, I have the time to answer it you don't." When they tell lies about me, they do me a favour. It gives me more grounds for my complaint.

Tonight Carol and I watched a film on television. When the film ended, it was Saturday. I had a cuppa-soup and some crackers and triangles. Carol and Vicki celebrated me coming off hunger strike by us all having a drink of hot chocolate. Carol gave me one of her bananas and I felt a lot better straight away. It was really strange that it was almost instantaneous how much better I felt. I never realised what a good food bananas were.

25   Life in Prison Deteriorates

Saturday, 16th April

Well, no visit today unfortunately. I had a letter to write, I needed to give my permission to my union representative for John to act/speak on my behalf in matters relating to my job. I intended to write him a brief note to that effect but ended up writing seven sides about my job, my responsibilities, the extra duties I had taken upon myself, the strain of being in 'special measures' and basically how I was not really coping. It was not work's fault, they would not have known. I had not told them but I tried to make the point that it was not really fair to sack me for an incident related to stress, when my job was a major cause of that stress.

The eggs never arrived for breakfast or lunch. The lunch was a saucer sized 'value' pizza which cost about 5p each. I ate a few of the hard but soggy lukewarm greasy frozen chips with it and a little of the slimy side salad. I was given a pear for desert but it was too hard to eat, it was of the usual lethal missile variety. I got some letters written to stave off the boredom and wrote John's birthday card which I had made and put it away ready for his birthday which I am going to miss.

It is on the 30th April. He says he's waiting till I am out to celebrate it.

Sunday, 17th April

Today I have absolutely nothing whatsoever to do except slit my throat. If I was at home I could be doing my spring cleaning and have my house like a sparkling new pin but I am here doing nothing while my home and family is neglected. John is out today with Oli, the weather looks nice and sunny so they should have a good day. Vicki works on the gardens and last week she emptied a bin from an office move and she found all sorts of things that have come in handy, like large brown envelopes and a roll of Sellotape. So I decided to cut up some of the cards that people had sent me, to make cards to send to family and friends to thank them, 'the girls' in particular, for all the campaigning they are doing on my behalf. They did Manchester on Wednesday and Urmston and Altrincham yesterday. Vicki made one each for her boys. I was pleased with the selection that I made and enjoyed making and writing them for people. It was light relief and very therapeutic.

Monday, 18th April

Today I put my letter to the governor into the office. I returned to education in the afternoon to give support in the basic literacy class. When I returned to the house a large envelope had arrived for me from John relating to my disciplinary hearing at work. I read all the documents regarding contract from the General Teaching Council and the Disciplinary Procedure from Salford Local Education Authority. There was a letter to me from Hazel Blears MP and one she had written on my behalf.

173

I deliberately did not read the report on me by the police to my employers as I had been told it was awful and I didn't want to upset myself before my visit, which is tomorrow.

Hazel Blears had written to Councilor Keith Mann at Salford Civic Centre.

"Mrs Walker is of course very keen indeed to retain her employment and has asked that there be a full and proper investigation into the circumstances surrounding her case and that she be given an opportunity to make full representations in any disciplinary process that may take place. It is of course important that all the proper procedures are followed in relation to Mrs Walker's case and I would be very grateful for your assurance that there will be a full investigation and that Mrs Walker will be afforded an opportunity both to participate in any disciplinary proceedings and to make full representations so that all the facts and circumstances of her case can be considered by the appropriate bodies. I look forward to hearing from you urgently with your assurances on this important matter."

Tuesday, 19th April

I got up quite excited today as I was having a visit from John, James and my dad this afternoon. I went to computer class as normal but on arriving back at the house at lunchtime I was called into the office. The resettlement officer was waiting to see me and he told me I was being 'shipped out' to HMP Buckley Hall tomorrow. He asked me to sign a slip to agree. I did not sign, I do not agree. I do not want to be moved. Why I am I being moved? I have just got to know people, made some friends and an established a routine. I told him I think I am being punished because I went on hunger strike. They don't want me dying here so they are shipping me out. He assured me that this was not the case, that if he wanted to punish me I would be going to Holloway. Well I may be going to Holloway when I go to London for my appeal. I have not seen John since my reception visit but this news has spoilt my visit with him now as I will have to tell him and I know he will be upset. I am not serving this sentence alone, my whole family is serving it with me and they are completely innocent.

When I got into visiting it was only John and James as my dad had forgotten his passport so had to wait outside. I told John about the move and we were both unhappy about it. It was not a good visit. There was a feeling of impending doom. Everything has gone wrong and it feels like I am never going to get out. Even when I arrange a visit people forget their passport or don't bother to ring and book according to the instructions. I am fed up with everybody and everything. When I returned to the house I read through the report from the police to my employer, Salford Local Education Authority (LEA), about the incident, my arrest and the offence. The report is very biased in its tone and contains a lot of lies, most of which I know I can prove to be so. I read it very carefully then with a pink pen which I borrowed from one of the other prisoners I underlined all the untrue or inaccurate statements. I then wrote what really happened in blue. I am not upset by it. It spurs me on to fight and prove them wrong. I feel strangely reassured because it is good evidence for my complaint. It is not necessarily the fault of the writer of the report, it is probably due to the information which he received. I suspect the DS, as the investigating officer, must have had some involvement. However if the Chief Inspector has taken it upon himself to write the report, the responsibility is his and he should also have taken it upon himself to ensure it was correct.

I found 47 inaccuracies in the report. These included the claim that the harassment at our home amounted to "a maximum of four incidents in a two year period". It said that the washing liquid container "had been discarded at the side of the car – it had been picked up and put on the car roof". In fact, it had been left outside our back door meaning that the assailant must have trespassed in our garden and there was no reference to the fact that its contents had been poured over the car. It said that I had walked 200 yards from the house before initially seeing the youths. There was no reference to the road sign being placed in the road. There was no mention of the youths 'fronting up' to me. It clearly stated that I shot at people. "Mrs Walker then discharged the gun between two and six times at the feet of one of the boys." Also: "She did confront the two boys; she did fire the pistol at them;" Implying that it was only by sheer good luck that I had missed and no-one was injured. The inaccuracies went on. It strongly implied that I was drunk. "... the fact she had been drinking alcohol the police were required to leave her for eight hours until she could be interviewed." My arrest report had clearly stated my condition as 'calm and sober.'

I decided to compile my own response, specifying the inaccuracies and challenging the unqualified opinions contained within the report, namely that I "lacked integrity" and "manipulated the media"! How could he say I lacked integrity when he had never met me? How did he think I could manipulate the media from the confines of prison when I barely had enough phone credit to keep in touch with my family?

Tonight I watched 'Holby City' on television. Someone lost a twin baby and nearly lost the other one. I thought again how lucky I was to have only been pregnant twice and have three gorgeous babies. I started to feel a bit more positive again. I phoned my daughter to tell her that we have no worries really because this short time is not important in the scale of things, not like the really important things in life like your health. I thought of my best friend Barbara whose partner Ibo is battling cancer. Donna told me that Robert starts his new job as an electrician on Monday. I am really pleased he deserves to get a good job.

I feel better after my phone call and have decided to treat my move to HMP Buckley Hall with the contemptuous indifference which it deserves.

26   High Security at Buckley Hall

HMP BUCKLEY HALL

Wednesday, 20th April

I was woken by an officer and got up at 8 a.m. I still did not know if I was going to HMP Buckley Hall today or staying at Styal. I was told by Chrissie that if I hadn't heard, I was going Then at 9 a.m. the officer told me that I was being taken over to reception at 9.30 a.m. to be taken to Buckley Hall. I phoned home and put it on the answer machine for John, where I was going. I wasn't bothered any longer, you are still are locked up wherever you are and it is not being with my family that is the worst thing. Some of the girls on the house were really nice though, I said goodbye to them and wished people luck.

I had served three weeks and two days at HMP Styal.

At reception I had my plastic bags searched and then repacked. I had the mandatory strip search by two officers, my clothes were searched and I redressed. I then had a cup of tea. Lorraine from our house, in for driving a getaway vehicle, made it for me as she works on reception. She obviously hadn't driven it fast enough. I didn't have time to finish it as the prison van arrived, there were four women including me on the 'ship out.' We left the prison through double security gates, the underneath of the van checked with mirrors, and we were on our way. It was nice to see the countryside, normal traffic and people's homes. I saw them in a different light now. They looked cosy and homely rather than just houses. The van driver drove really fast on the motorway as if he was frightened that we may get held up, and we arrived there in 40 minutes.

When we arrived it looked like a high security prison, with high dark grey metal fences topped with rolled razor wire and security lights on high metal posts. We traveled uphill through four set of gates and fences just to get to the reception, arriving at 11.30 a.m. We were let off the bus and checked in one by one, and then we waited in various rooms in between seeing various prison staff. When we were left we were locked in the rooms. The reception buildings are like large porta-cabins and painted grey. There is a grass verge and flower beds outside the reception. I later discover this is the only garden and is for the purpose of giving a good impression to visitors.

We individually saw an officer who questioned us about our offences and behavior, completing a sheet of tick box answers to questions like: – do you self harm? Name of offence in for? Do you have difficulty in controlling anger? A nurse from healthcare completed a health questionnaire, the mental health nurse a mental healthcare checklist. Our bags were checked again and we received our property in the statutory see-through plastic bag. We stayed in a locked room for an hour while staff had their lunch, then at 1.45 pm we were brought a packed lunch; a beef sandwich, biscuit and a breakfast pack. We were allowed a two minute call home each but when I rang no one was at home. It was nearly 4 p.m. and John and James were both still at work.

Eventually we were walked 'up the hill' to the induction wing. We passed through five more high metal security gates, set in the fences which are twenty foot high all topped with the same rolled razor wire. This is a 'very' high security prison with, we are told, "more cameras than the BBC." We passed the kitchen and college buildings which are a bit more substantial than the reception. The classrooms look like pebble dashed concrete porta-cabin's. The 'wings' are on the top of the hill. They are dark grey and look bleak and imposing with corrugated metal roofs. They are not named but lettered A to F. It was then that I realised the extent of what has been done to me!

When we entered they were traditional prison wings like Waite wing at Styal, two storey, metal landings, doors and lots of bars, just like you see on television prison programs like 'Porridge' and 'Bad Girls', which I believe was filmed at Buckley Hall. I asked for and was given a single cell. I was allocated cell 37 and I was escorted in. It was locked behind me I was told until 5.30 p.m. when I would be let out for tea. I started to write my diary. The cell is painted cream with a grey vinyl floor, it does not look clean although it is more modern than Styal. It is the size of one and a half box rooms and the metal door is painted pale green. The orange curtains at the small window are tied up, I untied them but then realised there is not enough light so I tied them up again. There is a single bed, the mattress doesn't look too thin, about three inches, but it is stained with period stains. I turned it over but it is just as bad so I made up the bed folding the bottom sheet double to give more protection from the mattress even though it is then not quite long enough. There is a sink and a toilet at the door end with a shower curtain. On the other wall is a lightwood veneer bedroom unit consisting of; television table, single wardrobe, writing desk and chair with three shelves over for books. There is a TV (thank god), a kettle which has to be placed on the floor to be plugged in and a hair dryer but no mirror.

The most upsetting thing is they have taken my eternity ring from me. I was not allowed to keep it here because it had stones in it. It was a present from John. When I was let out for tea the wing was busy, doors clanging and shouts echoing. I had to wait until last as people had pre-ordered their choice and I got what was left. All the chips had gone by this time. The prison officer sent for some more for me, so I ended up having a chicken leg in barbecue sauce with some really fresh hot chips. It was the best thing I had eaten since I got sent to prison. It was gorgeous. There are 60 cells on this wing, some take two prisoners, fifteen down each side top and bottom, connected by a metal landing and stairs. It is very busy, I do not know anyone but I am aware of their stares. They all seem young, there isn't anyone my age and I feel out of place and isolated. After tea there is an hour's association time but I stayed in my cell. We were then locked in. It is not like Styal where we still had the run of the house and could ring home at anytime. When I am locked in I work out the days to my appeal and start to tick them off. I am definitely going to go to London now.

Thursday, 21st April

I did not sleep well in the night although the beds are a lot better, more comfortable with a quilt rather than a blanket. My heart was pounding as if it was going to burst. If I had been at home I would have taken a diazepam tablet that the doctor had given me but I am not allowed them in here. My head has been itching all night and I need to make an appointment to see the nurse as I think I have got nits. The door was unlocked at 7.30 a.m. I got up and went down to ask for some cleaning fluid to clean the toilet (we cant have bleach). I had mopped the floor and wiped down the furniture last night so at least I feel the place is clean, when the toilet is cleaned.

The view from the window is bleak it looks like a concentration camp. The metal wings are grey and austere surrounded by the grey metal fences topped with the rolled razor wire. A cold wind blows on the top of the hill. They have just locked my door again it is 8.30 a.m. I don't know how long it is going to be locked for or what is going to happen to me today but I believe this is a 'working prison,' so someone may see me about what I am going to do. The people I have spoken to on this wing all seem to be going out the next day, next week, or in two or six weeks. No one here seems to be here for long. A lot seem to be in for shoplifting and I wonder why, if we are not dangerous, have we been put in such a high security place?

After an hour or so the cell is unlocked and I am taken out to begin the induction process. First we have a talk on 'domestics' by an inmate whose job it is to induct on this wing. She is young with long blonde hair and pretty and she looks like 'Sheila' in 'Shameless'. I believe she is a 'lifer'. We are then spoken to by a 'listener' who is trained by the Samaritans. She tells us about the prison listening service and shows us a video. We are then taken for the gym induction. I am not really interested in all the machines or volleyball etc. I would really like to do some swimming but that is not on offer. Whilst having demonstrations of the machines I start to be aware that I am having trouble getting a proper breath and I have pains in my chest. I feel increasingly stressed, like I didn't want to be there and have got to get out. In the end I can't help myself I just start to cry. I feel so stupid because I am amongst a group of people who I didn't even know. One of the girls who came in with me yesterday comforts me and looks after me, but I still don't really feel any better. I fear this place is making me mentally ill.

When we got back to the wing, I tell the prison officer and he contacts the health care on my behalf. He arranges for me to see the doctor but I am not sure when that will be. We are then locked in again until lunch. It is spaghetti bolognese which again is quite nice. Surprisingly, the mince was proper mince and didn't make you think of eye balls. I stay with the Liverpudlian girl who I came in with yesterday, who is looking after me despite that her children were taken off her for neglect. We went to her cell for a cup of coffee. Unusually we got a sachet in our breakfast pack. I then returned to my cell which is locked at 1.30 p.m. At 3.30 p.m. I am taken out of the cell to attend a basic literacy assessment. It was the same one I did at Styal. We are also told about the jobs available. I fancy doing hairdressing as I have always enjoyed it but am told I am not here long enough as it is a two year course, so it looks like I will have to return to the monotony of the computer class and helping with literacy again, unless I want to go packing things like tea bags or curtains. The man taking the class explained that prison life is about getting you back into the routine of work and teaching us skills for work. I don't need to be taught the routine of work; I have worked all my life. I have had three babies and only ever had two maternity leaves off work. I have the skills to work but I am not being allowed to because I am stuck in this hellhole. The classroom was cold and very dull and I was glad to get out of it. It typified the eerie and austere atmosphere of this whole place which is suffocating and because it is all metal it vibrates with every movement, so much so it seems to hum. I was glad to be locked in my cell again. I decided to write to John and tell him how awful this place is. I don't want to worry him further but I want him to know what they have done to me. I told him not to tell the children how awful it is though.

27   Anxiety and Despair

Thursday, 21st April continued ...

When the night is at its darkest the dawn breaks or so the
saying goes. Whilst queuing for my tea one of the inmates,
a friendly girl with a smiley face said that I have been on
television and that Tony Blair was going to apologise for me
being in prison, at 6 p.m. on Granada. I can't really believe that
is the case, but I ate my piece of bacon on a piece of sawdust
bread and went upstairs to my cell to watch Granada Reports.
It showed Tony Blair on his campaign trail, he is in Rochdale
and someone asked him about me. He said he felt very sorry
for me and that he was familiar with my case. He said his
party is the party tackling antisocial behavior but that he can't
interfere in decisions made by the courts.

My friends were also on the programme – Lynn and my
oldest school friend Barbara. They also had a spokeswoman
from, 'Mothers Against Guns' and asked Barbara to comment
on their campaign. I did not think this was very fair to our
Barbi, it was as if they presumed we were going to defend
having guns on the street. I hoped she wasn't going to have
one of her blonde moments when put in this predicament,

but she did brilliantly although she looked very perplexed. She said, "Well we're all Mothers against guns," which included me. Just because my friends were against me going to prison and did not think it was justified – does not mean they approved of me going out with weapons. When I phoned John he was angry about Tony Blair's comments. He said they all say a lot but nobody does anything! Sorry for me makes him look sympathetic but does not entail any action, anyway I am getting a visit on Sunday so that is good news. I had a bath in the eerie shared bathroom that has toilet paper stuffed in the keyhole! Then I was locked back in my cell at 8.30 p.m. till 7.30 a.m. the next morning.

Tony Blair is on again on the 10 p.m. news. He makes the same comments only more. He also said Hazel Blears has stepped in to ask Salford to postpone the hearing regarding my job so that I could speak for myself and present my case (thank God).

Friday, 22nd April

I was up before dawn to write to Tony Blair. I have had a bad night, I cannot stand the concentration camp atmosphere of this environment. I know they were evil far beyond this and I am not detracting from their evilness but that is the oppressive and eerie feeling that this environment creates.

I wrote to Tony Blair:

"I note on TV whilst on the election trail you spoke of my case and that you felt sorry for me. You certainly would feel sorry for me if you could see where they have put me. I have been put in a high security prison.

"The whole place is eerie and claustrophobic. It seems to hum/vibrate all the time."

I continued: "I can not bear to be here, I am having anxiety attacks where I can't breathe and have pains in my chest. I am waiting to see the doctor. He will have to prescribe something for me if they want me to cope here. It is making me mentally ill and I am worried that by the time I leave I will have become addicted to drugs. I dare not tell my children. Please help me. I have never hurt anyone in my life and only tried to protect my family. I can not cope with being shut in one of those white vans and locked in a box to come to London for my appeal unless I am drugged. My partner John is very angry. He says everyone is sympathetic but no-one does anything! Please will you do something or speak to someone who can. Please do it soon."

At 8.00 a.m. I rang John and it took seven calls to get through. John was very stressed, he says he is being mithered to death about Tony Blair by the press. He said I am here because I "kicked off", referring to my hunger strike. I told him to ring the solicitor and get her to ask the judge to reconsider my bail. Then I rang back to tell him I had written to Tony Blair but he was out. I rang six times. I was then locked back in my cell. At 9.30 a.m. I heard doors being unlocked, I thought: "What shit will I have to go to now!" I would rather just be left locked in here, but thank God, it was only a roll check.

I got back on the bed for a rest as I have not slept much. At about 11.30 a.m. the probation officer came to see me, it was part of the induction process. We went to his office. I enquired about getting a tag (HDC) which I could be eligible for on the 13th May, failing my being released on appeal on 4th May. I am not counting on anything any longer. I was given it in writing that I am not eligible because of my conviction but I already knew that. I wanted to know how my letter to the governor was going and how long it would take to hear if my plea of exceptional circumstances has been accepted or not. I am informed that the police are involved in the decision so that does not bode well for me. He also informed me that I am registered on the system as a 'POOPP' which is a 'Prolific Offender or Other Priority Prisoner' and showed me this on his computer screen! I didn't know what this meant but obviously it was a negative categorisation by its association with prolific offender, I just know if I don't win my appeal I am stuffed! I have never been in trouble in my life so I can not be a 'prolific offender', I must therefore be a 'priority prisoner' whatever that is? One who has complained about the police? One whose complaint is serious, so much so that it is being 'supervised' by the Independent Police Complaints Commission and one therefore who is subversive and must not be released early under any circumstances? Was it a ploy to keep me in until all the publicity had died down because they may not like what I had to say? The probation officer could not answer any of my enquiries. He gave me a notice of my release date. It is 28th June which seems a lifetime away I was then taken back to my cell following the interview. Although I have not been officially notified I am pretty sure that I will not now get approved for early release on a tag (HDC).

At about 3 p.m. the cell was unlocked and I was told I was going out on a tour of the prison. The officer introduced herself as my personal officer, Marcia. I told her I did not want to go. I had got the curtains shut so I couldn't see the prison blocks. I told her about my feelings for this environment, she tried to reassure me that it is really okay and better than Styal. I said she must be used to it, but that I find the atmosphere claustro-phobic, anyway she said the tour is compulsory and I had to go. I told her about my panic attacks and asked if I could see the doctor. She said that she would follow up my appointment.

I started to tell her that I have never hurt a fly and I do not deserve to be stuck here, but she has obviously heard it all before and it is water off a duck's back.

I went on the tour with the other girls who I came in with and a prison officer who seemed a bit vacant as if she had other things on her mind, but was pleasant enough. We went into the chapel, which is part of the gym building and built out of breezeblocks, charcoal grey, but emulsioned white inside the chapel. The minister who spoke to us is a lady Methodist minister. She is about my age and grey haired and told us it is a peaceful place to come and pray. I asked her: "Will it help me to forgive the investigating DS and stop me wanting to set his police car on fire, with him in it?" I am in a bad mood today. I hate it here. I can't stand it any longer. She just laughed, nervously. On the way out, she said: "It must be hard for you, an old woman with all these young ones." I thought: "God, I must look ancient, I am only 48." She told me she was there if I needed anyone to talk to. I tried to smile politely and thank her for her offer.

We had a tour of the rest of the 'concentration camp' and went back through five locked gates in the high security fences to the reception and visiting area. Am I really that dangerous that I require to be locked up in somewhere like this? Do I look like I could get over even one 20ft high fence? I am sure they could be using their resources a lot better. They say prisons are overcrowded, well no wonder, do I really require this level of security? The convictions I have imply that I do. I am starting work at the education block on Monday and we also visit this. As we walked back to Stallag 14, the sunshine was lovely. I thought of all the lovely places I could be walking and all the lovely people I could be with, rather than being in here.

When I got back I phoned home. John kept talking in

riddles. I think his head has gone and he has lost the ability to make rational conversation. He is worried about me and is all in a muddle but I was in such a bad mood that I couldn't be bothered trying to understand what he was telling me. I told him I was not wasting my credit on twaddle that I don't understand and would phone him again later. He was rambling on about the kids and their cars and who is insured for what car, which is something I always sort out. I don't have enough credit for people to explain themselves properly, especially when I am talking to a halfwit. I am feeling very grumpy and do not have any patience whatsoever.

I phoned Donna and she is really looking forward to visiting on Sunday, bless her. That cheers me up a bit. I watched Corrie then phoned the halfwit again but he was no better. The domestic details of life are becoming overwhelming for him. John cannot cope when he is under pressure and loses all sense of order and organisation. Because I am not coping, he is not coping. He is serving my sentence and still going to work as well as trying to do the washing, ironing, cooking, cleaning, shopping, looking after James and my dad as well as communicating with all the well wishing supporters, friends and press. We normally work as a team. I do the domestic and kids stuff and John does the practical and technical things. Everything has lost its equilibrium because I am in here and what good is it doing anyone for me to be locked up?

28 Suspicion and Oppression

Saturday, 23rd April

I feel a bit better and more in control today after the stress and anxiety of the move. I still think the reason I was moved was strange. There were girls on that house at Styal who had requested, almost begged to come here because it is nearer to their families. I have decided that my priority is to look after myself so I am fit to continue my fight for justice and go home to my family. So I had a shower and asked again about my doctor's appointment for the third day running. I have also decided to have some breakfast as my weight loss has been too rapid. As a teacher of nutrition I am aware of the dangers of this, that it weakens muscle and that the heart is a muscle which can be weakened. My heart has been pounding with anxiety attacks, which is why I have asked to see the doctor. My grandma died of a heart attack after she lost a stone slimming in a short period of time. My weight on entry to this prison was 85 kilos and it was 90 on entry to Styal. I think I have lost even more now and although I am no lightweight by any stretch of the imagination, this rate of weight loss is too fast and I need to look after myself for the sake of my family.

I keep telling myself that the important thing is who you are, not where you are. It is easy to lose a sense of who you are in here and be a number rather than a person. I have decided that if I can get over the domineering effect of the physical reality that is this prison, I can cope. I just need to get my mindset into 'prison mode'. I am here, I can't do anything about it. If I let it stress me I am only hurting myself and my family.

Cell doors are not locked today as it is Saturday. People have been milling about the Wing having a chat. The girls here are friendly enough but they are not really on my wavelength. They seem to know everything there is to know about the law though, they assure me my sentence would not be altered in a negative way due to it being my first offence. As I sit here next to the barred 2ft by 3ft window, I notice all the dents in the light green gloss painted metal door where it has been punched and head butted, probably when it was a men's prison. I phone John this evening. He is still very stressed because he can't find what I have asked him to bring in for me tomorrow, namely pyjamas and t-shirts. Tonight I am writing to Salford LEA to answer the charges brought against me of gross misconduct that could result in dismissal from my job. If upheld I could be sacked without notice. Life seems one battle after another at the moment. Will it ever come to an end?

Sunday, 24th April

This morning was a bad morning. I was not as strong as I vowed I would be yesterday and felt a bit wobbly in the chest and near to tears. I was so glad my family were coming this afternoon. I worried I would upset them though like I upset John last night. I washed my hair and got ready then was escorted down with a group of other prisoners.

My visit was lovely. Donna, Craig and John came. I had lovely hugs and squeezed and kissed them all. They are so gorgeous. Craig told me that he has failed his final assignment at college! I said he'd better make sure he took up his offer of a place in nursing from the Manchester School of Nursing because he wouldn't get another offer. He got an unconditional offer because he is clever and gets fantastic reports from his placements at the hospital. I thought that maybe he had failed his assignment because of all this carry on and how upset he has been.

Donna said everyone at school sends their love and she has been busy with the website. We discussed the petition that the girls are doing. It will have to go to London before the appeal because after will be too late. John says he needs to sort this out with 'the girls', my friends. It all needs to be co-ordinated but I am normally the organiser. John said it is 'manic' at home. The phone rings all the time with reporters wanting the latest update. He has not said anything about me being moved or that I am having anxiety attacks because we have already been accused of 'manipulating the press' and they will think I am trying to get sympathy so we are saying nothing. I got lovely kisses and cuddles from them before they went home and I came back to my cell a happy woman. After tea I phoned to have a chat with James as only three can come on a visit and he had to stay at home. I later learned that they were very worried after this visit because apparently I was so weird; they knew I wasn't coping in that horrible place but had pretended everything was alright and I was normal because they didn't want to upset me. They just hoped I would be freed soon before any permanent damage was done.

Monday, 25th April

Today I did my first morning as an orderly in the education unit. I am in an 'English as a second language' class. The teacher is called Ann and is French. The education block is a prefabricated type of concrete building. It is dull and cold. There doesn't seem to be anywhere in this prison that gets any sunshine at all. In the afternoon I had my first IT class in this prison. The teacher is called Chrissy and is a bit older than me. I said I wanted to improve my keyboard skills so she set me to work on a typing software package. I am feeling a bit happier today after my lovely visit yesterday but I can't talk to John as I get locked in at 8.30 p.m. and he doesn't finish work until 9 p.m. on Mondays. So this evening I am going to ring Donna. Looking forward to the phone calls to my family keeps me going.

Tuesday, 26th April

I got my appointment (at last) with the nurse today, for 10 a.m. When I got up I was told to pack up my things and that I wouldn't be going to 'work' this morning. I was moving. I packed everything in a clear plastic sack ready to move to C Wing next door. I feel a bit apprehensive in case some of the women are unsavoury. When I saw the nurse, I explained about the anxiety attacks, chest pains and getting upset. I told her about my concerns about going to London in one of those small cells in the white van, and getting claustrophobic and bout my worries regarding the appeal and that I couldn't stand the thought of effectively being 'sent down' for a third time. The first time I didn't know what to expect. When I didn't get bail pending my appeal, and I thought I was going home, I couldn't eat, I felt so let down and distressed. If I go all the way to London, sit through another court case, and then get sent back to prison to serve longer than I already have done, I will miss my twin boys' eighteenth birthday and fear that I will fall to bits. I told the nurse that I don't think I can cope without something from the doctor. She gave me an appointment to talk to the doctor this evening.

At tea time the other inmates seemed friendly enough. A lot of them have the vacant eyes that I have seen before though while being in prison and that is a bit depressing. I did not get to see the doctor after waiting for one and a half hours. The nurse explained that although I did have a slip, I was not put on the list and they are "choc-a-block." She asked if I could come back tomorrow and I agreed. I haven't exactly got anything else on my social calendar. I just want the doctor to give me something to get me through the weekend now.

I received a bundle of mail from Styal today, more letters of support and disgust at the government. Also letters from friends: Barbara, Janet, Bev and Christine, the 'Free Linda' campaigners. They have received the cards I sent them. I am very touched by Barbara's letter. She says she is 'thinking about me' then says: 'can't really think about anything else'. When I rang John at tea time he said the press are starting to show more interest again as the appeal approaches. When they ring he tells them I am fine. He is frightened to tell them that I am not fine and that I have been moved. John told me the girls are getting the petition together to send to London by recorded delivery. I am so grateful to everyone who is working to free me and for the support of the public. It keeps me going when things seem hopeless.

Wednesday, 27th April

I woke up early, it was just getting light so must have been around 6.45 a.m. I wake up early every day, if I could sleep longer I could sleep away my sentence, but I can't. I don't go to sleep until midnight because I can't sleep unless I am tired and then I wake up really early. I do not get tired because I do nothing all day, except sit about suffering from anxiety and terminal boredom. I took the hairdryer back to the girl in the opposite cell. Even though I am trying not to mix with people here a lot of them are showing me a lot of kindness. When last night I asked to borrow a dryer people fell over themselves to get one for me. Someone gave me an extra brew pack at tea time and on Sunday, when I couldn't have my writing pads from John because they were not sealed in a cellophane pack, one of the girls gave me a pad. Other prisoners recognise who I am and if they say anything they support me and think it is wrong that I am here.

I went over to 'meds' after lunch, as I needed some tablets which I only take when I am on a period. I told the nurse what I took when I came in last Wednesday and she said they were in stock, however when I went over they had not got any which I am not happy about. If I were at home I would have them in, but that responsibility is taken away as is every other decision about your life and you have absolutely no autonomy.

This time next week I could be free, but I am too frightened that I may not be, to think about it. The nice tea I had on the first night must have been a blip, it has got gradually worse since and tonight's was awful; two value sausages and a boiled egg served still in the shell with sawdust bread. At least I have been able to have a few brews today because of the extra tea bags and milk I was given yesterday, even if the tea does tastes like tree bark. Some people don't seem to notice the food is horrible; they shovel it all down and get fatter and fatter, because there is a lot to eat if you want it but it is all 'stodge.' I gave away a piece of chocolate butter cream cake and a piece of cake for supper that looked like very solid Madeira cake with some dried fruit in.

When I saw the doctor at 6.30 p.m., he put me on tranquilizers or at least that's what I think they are. He wouldn't give me the diazepam that my own doctor had given me as we are not allowed 'mood changing' drugs. He said the tablets would calm me down for the transfer to Holloway. The prison vans are so cold I will probably be dead of hypothermia by the time I get to London at my age. He prescribed the tablets for twice a day but I don't want to take them all the time, I would rather just be able to take one when I need one. He said they will keep my head clear for the appeal, so I will know all about it when they send me down for a third time!

Thursday, 28th April

At 8 a.m. I went for my tablets. I do feel calmer but not happier about being in here. I do not have a lot to do now, I have written all my letters and prepared statements; one for if I am released and another for if I am not. Time is passing really slowly, I waited for 2 p.m. when I had a legal visit from my barrister and Sue Ann about the appeal, seven days later than planned. But when it is time to go I end up being late because of a 'lock down.' This happens when prisoners are counted but the figures don't balance and someone must have been missing. I am going to try to get my diaries out to them in a file of papers about the appeal. I am worried about having my writing here and taking it to Holloway in case it goes missing somewhere along the way. So many peculiar things have happened to me; like not getting bail pending appeal, not hearing about my HDC and being classified as a POOPP. They have regular 'cell spins' which are a full search of the cell for forbidden items and I worry that if my diaries are found they will be seen as 'propaganda' or 'a breach of security.' Such is the atmosphere of oppression.

At my legal visit I raised a few points with my barrister that keep getting repeated in court and that are incorrect. It was not police witness 2 who came up our path with police witness 1. I never carried the rifle over my shoulder but broken open across my arm. The pistol was not loaded, I did not know it, but it was stated by John on oath and John does not tell lies. I told her it was not an accident that no one got hurt but my intention. My barrister tells me she thinks the judge will take the public opinion into account and it sounds like he wants to reduce my sentence, from what is said in the bail refusal notice, but she said it could go either way. She told me: "They are a law unto themselves", he may want to make an example of me. She said I must prepare myself and that they may "send me down" again! I said: "Just give it your best shot, remind them it is damaging my health, it is punishing my completely innocent family and it is cruel." She said she would do her best. I told her that I had written to apply for HDC on grounds of "exceptional circumstances". My barrister said if my circumstances weren't exceptional she didn't know what was.

She showed me my prison reports from Styal and from here at Buckley Hall. Styal have given me a lovely report, but here they have said I have been rude to staff, called someone an 'idiot' and refused to cooperate in induction. She said if the conviction is quashed the judge may order a retrial. After the visit I spoke to staff about the report, they said they could not imagine that I would be rude to anyone and would check my records. I thought you would do better to ask Marcia, the officer who had not been impressed by my protestations. When I rang John he said he knew I hadn't said that because 'idiot' was not a word that I use.

29   About to be Clinically Insane

Friday, 29th April

The girls, my campaigners, were on breakfast television, getting ready to put the petition in. They said they had 9,000 signatures. Apparently a man called David Davies and his wife Margaret from Barrow-in-Furness in Cumbria who I don't even know had collected 1200 of these! I went to education for the morning English class. The teacher talked about housing, house programmes on TV and housing issues in general. I thought this could be my last class and I really hoped it was. I have had enough of education for life. I had had enough of it about four years ago. The bank holiday weekend lay ahead. By Tuesday I will have to be in Holloway, to be in London for my appeal on Wednesday. I don't want to come back here for two more months and see all the Spring slip away from me. We have paid to put our caravan in Anglesey and I want to be there. We have not been able to enjoy the van yet, because of all the problems we have had at home, and we were looking forward this year to being able to go with peace of mind. Now we had found out who was targeting our home and why, it had ceased.

After the class I asked the teacher if she could please contribute to my reference. I told her what the first one, after one day, had said and she said she definitely would. I asked could she do it today because of the short time scale and as we spoke she saw Mark one of the junior governors who was responsible for resettlement. He was only young, 30ish, medium build with gingery hair. He was in the hall outside the room and she said that we will talk to him now. Ann said to him if anyone were to be asked for a reference it should be her, as I had worked with her. She said she would do one today and give it to him. He spoke to me and said it had been very difficult for him because he had been asked after only one day. I told him I would never be rude to staff and certainly had never called anyone an idiot. I said I had had an anxiety attack during induction and did not want to do the tour of the prison because of the effect it had on me, but was told it was compulsory, so I had complied. I told him I could not cope with the high security environment and found it claustrophobic and that I was on tranquilizers from the doctor. He asked about the incident and where I lived and worked because he knew the area and one of my neighbours. I told him about my boys, their jobs and how these vandals had started to target them. He said he would get another report done now that he had more information to go on. I asked him about my worry, that if I did not get released on appeal that I would have to come back here and I didn't like it. He wished me luck and said if that happened then it would have to be looked at then but hopefully it would not.

Today at lunchtime I received a letter forwarded from the governor at Styal regarding my application for HDC. It had been refused. It is a good job I have taken my tablet because I fear it may have given me a heart attack the state I am in at in at the moment. I rang Sue Ann to tell her a couple more points; that I have now lost a stone and that I had just seen on the television that the girls had 9,000 signatures. She informed me it was now nearer to 10,000 as Chris, my brother, had got more as had Donna, Craig and John.

Whilst in education this afternoon staff must have been discussing me at lunchtime because they were saying "good luck" and that they may not see me again after the Bank Holiday. Ann had said make sure I said goodbye to her but I don't want to tempt fate so I said: "Thank you for writing my reference."

I found out when I went for my tablet that they were 'propranolol' and are a beta-blocker for anxiety, to stop the heart racing and chest pains. They are not anti-depressants. Two days ago whilst I was waiting to see the doctor a girl was speaking to me about me being her mum's hero. She said she had shared a kitchen at HMP Durham with Rose West. I was really shocked at the level of the circle of acquaintance that I had been reduced to, spooked actually and very unnerved. I decided that I only wanted to stay in my cell from now on. I hoped that the two girls sharing the next door cell would not keep banging on my wall tonight, I thought it was perhaps because I had the TV on but when I turned it off they still had theirs on? I received another pile of letters from Styal today, about twenty including a lovely one from Donna spurring me to keep strong and one from Oli and Nicky, John's son and his girlfriend.

Saturday, 30th April

I had a really bad night last night, I woke up twice with a very funny feeling in my chest. John had said that beta-blockers give you funny side effects and it has made me frightened. I feel like a hypochondriac but I am really worried I may have a heart attack like my grandma who died after losing weight too quickly. This plays on my mind. I don't want to die before I see my family again I need to see my family and I do not know when that will be. I may die of anxiety and never see them again!

The morning came and I have nothing to look forward to now for the Bank Holiday weekend that stretches before me. The prospect of this weekend, with the uncertainty that lies at the end of it for me seems intolerable and never ending. I rang John to wish him a happy birthday; he has received his cards but I have nothing to tell him. I lay on the bed with the Saturday morning cookery programmes on and to my surprise I had a bit of a doze. I then realised I had not been for my tablet, so got up to ask the officer but I had missed 'meds' and could not now have my tablet. To be honest I am relieved, the effects of the tablets were worrying me more than the symptoms for which I was taking them. I got back on my bed and dozed the rest of the morning away which I hate, I am always busy with at least one project on the go at home.

At 11 a.m. we are locked up for a roll count and unlocked at 12 noon for the cooked breakfast we get on a Saturday. We were locked straight back up to eat it in our cells until afternoon association time. The weather was dull which I was glad about. It is worse being in here when it looks nice. They do not seem to search the cells as much on this wing. When I was on the induction wing they searched the cells a minimum of twice a day and often four times. They are supposedly done at random.

Whilst I have been writing my diary the lunchtime local news has come on about my petition. 'The girls' are on the television:- Barbara, Janet, Jan, Joyce, Lisa, Lynn, Sarahlee, Jill,

Bev and Irene. Bev Hughes my MP is also with them. They are presenting the petition which now has over 10,000 signatures to the Minister for Prisons, Paul Goggins. He speaks about me and says he does not know me but that everyone who does tells him I am a fine upstanding member of the community who does a valuable job and does not deserve to be sent to prison. It is lovely to see them all on TV as it seems ages since I have seen them in person.

It is now the evening. This afternoon passed really slowly. Some of the girls on the wing asked me to play a game, I didn't really fancy it but I joined in. We played 'Who wants to be a Millionaire' and 'Black Jack.' I know they don't have long to go to get out so they can't have done anything very serious. The mail was given out whilst we were playing and I got an answer from 10 Downing Street in reply to the letter I sent to Tony Blair last week. The girls were very impressed, one said if she had got that she would frame it!

It was marked from the 'Direct Communications Unit'. It said: "Dear Mrs Walker, I am writing on behalf of the Prime Minister to thank you for your letter of 22 April. This is receiving attention. Yours sincerely, W Argyle."

We got a salad sandwich for tea with rocket, cucumber and tomato tops. Some of the inmates thought they were being fed dandelion leaves. The 'Free Linda Campaigners' were on Granada news at 6 p.m. Bev Hughes my MP spoke on my behalf. She said that although what Linda did was not right, the fact that she had gone to prison makes a 'mockery' of the British justice system. The petition was handed to the minister for prisons who said my appeal was not far off and hopefully I would be home soon. I felt a lot less stressed now, now that I have had all this attention and publicity for my case. I am beginning to feel a little bit more confident again. I went for my tablet but I didn't take it. I kept it down the side of my mouth and then retrieved it, after my bad experience last night. I now have one if I need it.

Sunday, 1st May

I try to stay in bed as long as possible to make the day shorter but unfortunately I woke up. The girls in the next door cell, who were only messing about the other night, they were apparently knocking to ask, "'ave you gort my: sheep/ combine harvester/ tractor?" as if they were a Cornish farmer but I was not in the mood to be mad. Anyway they knocked and offered me their TV pages so I could select my viewing, which I did. They also lent me their mop and bucket with Lenor in it, to mop my room so it smells nice. I can not get any of these things because I have been moved and have to work a week in hand before I can have 'canteen' which means, spend your wages. My wages are £7.50 a week in education and up to £20 maximum can be transferred from private money. I only really want phone credit anyway and thankfully I have still been able to get the phone credit by special application. The door was unlocked for a few hours this afternoon and I sat out of my cell for a change. I got talking to some girls at the table. They all gave me coffee, sugar, sweets and milk because they realised I haven't got anything with not being able to order 'canteen'. I showed them my photos of family. Natalie from the next cell showed me her poem, it was about drugs and how her addiction got her into crime and ruined her life. It is very sad and moving.

I phoned John. He has been making arrangements for going to London with Donna Craig and my dad. They are leaving Tuesday evening at 5 p.m. to stay the night in London. If I don't go home with them they will be devastated, John has been doing the vacuuming, bless him! Only one more day to go here then I move to Holloway!

30   HMP Holloway

Monday, 2nd May

At 1.30 p.m. I am told: "Get to reception with your stuff." I thought: "Yes! I am on my way!" As I was asking: "Am I going now or is it just to take my stuff to reception?" I saw Chrissie who was in the next room on Barker House. She is on the induction wing next door. We had a brief chat through the bars at the door. She said, "I got my tag," meaning her approval for HDC, and that she got moved there two days ago. I told her: "I'm on my way" and she said: "You'll get it, good luck". I thanked her and tried to tell her I had enquired about her dog, who she was worried about – John's daughter Rachel works for the RSPCA – but she was shut back in before I could finish telling her that he was OK.

I got to the reception and took my things, leaving some, pyjamas toiletries and clothes, for tomorrow. I had to wait at the gates to be let through then wait in reception to have my things checked off my list to make sure I hadn't got anyone else's. By the time I got back I had missed outside association so I couldn't talk to Chrissie and I am off first thing in the morning. Still, it was nice to see her face – she is a really nice girl. I have planned my viewing for tonight, it is Corrie, Airline and Corrie again, that is it really. When I get home I am going to give up watching telly (except for Corrie). I rarely watch it anyway but sometimes I felt like I was missing something. The truth is I wasn't missing anything really, but it has helped to keep me sane in here.

I am locked in now prior to tea. I have just knocked on the wall to next door to tell Natalie and Allison I am off in the morning. They said "good luck". This will be my last tea here I really hope.

Time for bed now – hopefully my last one in here. The tea was really horrible, two sausage that looked still pink and wobbly. I ate one with some overcooked cauliflower and a roast potato. We were given an ice cream that was actually a recognizable make, a Del Monte mango and passion sorbet on a stick. It felt like a party.

I phoned John at home. He has been to my brother's barbecue for his birthday but came home in time for me to ring before 'bang up' at 8.30 p.m. He is a love and I am missing him terribly. He was getting sorted for going to London tomorrow and says he hopes I am coming home with them and I do to. I hope this is my last night here. I said I'll ring tomorrow first thing if I get chance, if not by the time I arrive at Holloway he will have left so I took the mobile number down on a bit of paper and put it in my glasses case. We said good night and see you soon! God, I hope so!

The officer who came to lock the cell put his head in and said: "You're going to London are you"? I said: "Yes". He said: "Good luck" and I thanked him. That was really nice of him. I daren't think about feeling confident but I definitely don't feel as worried. I feel trepidation tinged with excitement.

Tuesday, 3rd May

I am sat in my cell ready to go; hair washed, bed bunked, rubbish bagged, bag packed. I have been given a note to see the nurse at 8 a.m. to be checked as fit to travel. The girls next door were knocking when I pressed the taps to wash my hair because they make a noise but I knocked back and said: "Sorry but got to get ready to go to London." They said: "Don't worry, use the taps if you want, and "Good luck". They sounded nearly as excited as me.

As soon as my cell was unlocked I rang John to tell him I am on my way. I went across to the medical centre to see the nurse. Everyone was wishing me luck. I met the three Liverpudlians's I came in with and got hugs. I got called in straight away. The nurse to asked: "Are you okay?" I said: "Yes." So she said: "Okay off you go then, that's all I need, good luck". That was it. A prison officer took me through the five fences down to reception and on the way he told me he hoped my appeal was successful and that I shouldn't be here. I waited about ten minutes, then the rest of my possessions were checked out and ticked off my list. I was then locked in a holding room to wait for the van. After about twenty minutes I was called in for the strip search. I was asked if I had anything I shouldn't have and I said: "Yes." I had kept the tablet – the beta blocker. I asked could I keep it in case I needed it on the van but it was taken off me. They said if I was not okay to let the guard know, I thought: "I am going to be okay because I can't wait to get out of this horrible oppressive place." I had to wait for about ten more minutes in the locked holding room. I was then let out to get on the van. Only four more fences to go through,

I asked: "Are we going straight there or around the world?" The guard said: "Straight there, no stops". I felt happier about that. There was only me on the van with the driver and the guard, both ladies. We slowly made our way stopping and starting through the gates getting checked, I presumed. I could see out of the 1 ft square window but it made everything look brown. It looked like Spain with all the foliage burnt by the sun. The soil looked brown like grit sand, I watched as we drove away through Rochdale and down to the motorway.

I had served one week and six days in HMP Buckley Hall.

I got a bit worried when I realised we were heading north not south but we went to Leeds and got on the M1. The van went like the clappers passing everything in sight. We must have been going at least 80 or 90mph. We got on the M1 at Leeds at 9.30 a.m. and came off at Watford at 12.30 p.m.. I did not realise we were not actually there but there was a coach turned over ahead so we had come off on a detour and then got back on further up. Holloway is quite near central London I think, because I recognized all sorts of 'Fools and Horses' landmarks like the Camden Road and the like. We arrived about 2 p.m. after the detour. I sat in the van while the paperwork was checked, Holloway is where the last woman was hanged in this country, Ruth Ellis. Her sentence had also caused a public outcry and was instrumental in the abolition of capital punishment in this country.

Holloway has a lot nicer atmosphere than Buckley Hall. For a start it is in a town not on the moors like a concentration camp. It is built in red brick. We drove through one large metal gate with no razor wire, which raised up for us to enter. This led into a courtyard, where I was taken into reception. It was very light and friendly. My bag was checked in and I was strip searched again. I was then asked to sit in the holding room and told I could have a cup of tea. I was left in the room although it was unlocked, very civilized, and I was made a lovely cup of tea that didn't taste like tree bark. I sat and waited to see the nurse in the bright and airy room. Large windows without bars were open, the sun streamed in and I could see gardens and hear birds. It was almost like a hotel but behind front of hotel. The governor came to introduce himself to me. He knew who I was. He shook my hand and wished me luck. He was very nice and friendly like all the staff seem to be, but mainly the place is not oppressive.

I saw the nurse and my blood pressure was fine at 138/ 85 – a lot better than when I came in to Styal. She gave me a lovely big tube of moisturizer. I knew that John, dad, Donna and Craig were leaving at 5 p.m. At 4 p.m. I asked if I could use the phone and the PO got my phone credit sorted. I caught them just as they were already about ready for off. They are staying over. I am very happy that I will be seeing them soon even if it will only be across the court room.

When I was taken up to the wing it was like a block of flats, about four storeys high. This wing is more like a hospital ward than a prison wing, no metal landings and stairs and wooden doors. It is sparse but it has a whole different atmosphere. When I look out of the window in my cell I look down onto gardens and pigeons. It is walled in brick, the wall is high but the flats that surround it are at about the same height as the prison and I can see people's homes, normal homes of people not in prison. It makes me feel less isolated. I went for tea in the sunny dining room and could have a cheese salad which was very nice and fresh. I asked if I would be able to have a hair dryer in the morning and I was told: "No, you can have it tonight." So I had a bath and washed my hair. It will be all stuck up by morning. I am going to watch the TV until I am really tired or I will never sleep. There is no privacy in this cell as it is next to the office and I can hear telephones and radios. There is an open box like a large post box with no flap in the door. The toilet is right next to the hole.

Wednesday, 4th May

I was woken at 6 a.m. and given a cup of hot water to make a cup of tea. I was washed, dressed and ready for 6.30 a.m. I will be going out through reception with the usual checks and then in a prison van, but I do not think we are far out of London. I feel like Dick Whittington. I can not eat any cereal like I did yesterday as I am too nervous. I daren't even think I may be on my way home soon. My statements, prepared ready for both eventualities, are rolled up in my glasses case. I just hope that I will be reading one of them out personally. I am now waiting to be taken out of my cell.

31   So Close Yet So Far Away

At around 6.45 a.m. I was taken down to reception with two officers and a group of prisoners who were also attending court. The sunshine once again streamed through the windows in the reception area. It was a bright and fresh spring morning which I hoped was a good omen. I waited for about 40 minutes, now used to waiting around. I remember thinking: "What will my family be doing now?" and how close by they must be. After undergoing the mandatory strip search, which I was getting quite used to by now, I was taken into a van and we were on our way to the Royal Courts of Justice.

After first dropping other prisoners at other courts, we eventually arrived late at the Royal Courts of Justice. We entered through large white wooden gates at the rear of the courts. Once through the gates I assumed I would have been out of sight but a picture did later appear in a newspaper of me entering the court – 'double handcuffed' to a guard. Inside, I was put in a small waiting room and offered a cup of tea. It felt very civilized to be made a cup of tea. The staff were very friendly and told me I had been on the morning news. Some came to wish me luck. I had already received so many letters from strangers but to have such encouragement in person was reassuring. I was then taken into another room to meet my barrister and Sue Ann.

We discussed the judgement and I gave her some notes which I had jotted down on a piece of paper. 'Not a shred of evidence that these were the youths,' now disproved. I particularly wanted her to get the point across that it was not an accident that no-one was injured, it was my intention. She informed me that the police had been listening to my telephone conversations whilst I was in prison and that I had supposedly threatened to shoot Eleanor Moritz, the reporter from the BBC, when I was released. This must have been in the conversation I had with John when he had given her an interview on our front drive. It was never meant to be taken seriously and John would have known this.

John had told me, whilst I was in HMP Styal, that he suspected our phone at home had been tapped because it kept clicking but I had dismissed this and told him he was paranoid. I said it was ridiculous to imagine I was really that important to warrant such a level of surveillance. I told her I had made some choice comments regarding the investigating DS, that he wore "pervy glasses" and was an "ugly ginger git," just in case John was right. Sue Ann told me that one of the three High Court Judges hearing the case was Lord Justice Rose and that he was: "one of the top judges in the land". Then they wished me good luck before ringing the bell to be let out.

The two guards who escorted me into court both wished me luck. One said: "You'll walk, don't worry." I thought it must be unusual for so many people who worked in a court to be wishing good luck to the prisoner. Another good omen I hoped, I still did not want to raise my hopes though. As I walked down the narrow corridor, I remember a heavy sense of foreboding at my fate being in the hands of others, faceless people who knew nothing about me. The worst thing I thought that could happen now would be that I would have to serve the remaining eight weeks of my sentence but that, at this moment, seemed like an eternity to me.

I had served five weeks and two days in custody.

As I stepped like an animal into the caged dock in the ornately decorated court, I was faced with three well-dressed, red-robed judges. I glanced at the public gallery which was very full. I could see John, Donna, Craig and my dad. I knew that a lot of the others would be reporters. Lord Justice Rose began by saying that the case being heard was an appeal. He said the application for leave to appeal the convictions was dismissed but the application to appeal on sentence was upheld. At that moment, I didn't care about the convictions. I just wanted to be released.

My barrister then stood up to present her case. She appeared nervous, possibly due to her relative youth and inexperience and Lord Justice Rose seemed to prompt her. Then to my surprise, he interrupted her, saying: "Can I just say Ms Arshad, the appropriate sentence is a Conditional Discharge." I knew I had heard what I longed to hear but I hardly dared to believe it. I mouthed to the guard: "Does that mean I am going home?" She said: "Yes." Relief flooded through my body and I relaxed at last. I looked around me and took in the magnificence of the occasion. Everything seemed bright and colourful in contrast to the gloom which had hung over me since I had been sent to prison and during the difficult times before that. The court was beautifully decorated; some of the press were sneaking out to report that I was being freed. My family were all smiling at me. They were as relieved and excited as me.

My barrister then continued to present the case for my appeal against the sentence. I remember thinking how brave she was as she eloquently presented the case and kept her composure despite the added pressure of the media hanging on her every word. I was trying to take in the news that I had longed for but had not dared to think about. I was surprised to see the prosecution barrister sitting there in his gown and wig. I would have thought he would have wanted to keep a low profile after the things he had said at the trial, now disproved. He did not contribute to the proceedings, I suppose because the convictions were upheld he felt vindicated. Neither did he object to my release. By the time Lord Justice Rose began to speak I was ready to listen again. I wanted to take in every word, the words that would send me home.

He said: "For some time prior to the 14th August 2004 the appellant and her family had been subjected to a number of incidents taking place at their home, including two burglaries, criminal damage, thefts and nuisance telephone calls. The appellant believed that the incidents were connected with each other and demonstrated a campaign of harassment against her and her family." He went on: "The facts are conveniently rehearsed by the learned Recorder when he passed sentence."

He went on to repeat Recorder Browne's comments at the sentencing before passing comments about why he was refusing leave to appeal against the conviction.

"The appellant seeks to appeal against conviction on a single ground, namely, the availability of fresh evidence in the form of two statements from Mr David Matthews, who was the appellant's milkman. Leave is sought to adduce that evidence on the basis that, had it been heard by the jury, it might have made a difference to their verdicts and therefore the convictions of the appellant are said to be unsafe.

"We declined to admit that evidence for three principal

reasons: first, it is on its face of questionable value. The two statements are, in several respects, inconsistent with each other and both show obvious uncertainties. Furthermore, the two events described as having occurred in about April 2004 were not of such significance to Mr Matthews as to cause him to tell anyone (including the appellant) about either of the until nearly a year later, in February 2005, after the appellant had been convicted at trial.

"Secondly, on the assumption that Mr Matthew's account of events is correct, it simply does not support an assertion that —— (PW 1) was responsible for any damage to or vandalism of the appellant's property. At best, the second incident described, suggesting that —— (PW 1), contrary to his evidence before the jury, had been to the appellant's house on an occasion in April 2004, could, as seems to us, only bear on —— (PW 1)'s credit. Evidence bearing solely on credit is not, save in exceptional circumstances which do not arise in this case, admissible.

Thirdly he stated that what Mr Mathews had witnessed in April threw no light upon what happened at the time the firearm was discharged. He went on:

"It is therefore, as it seems to us, inconceivable that had the jury been permitted to hear what appears in those statements, their verdict might have been different. Accordingly, the proffered evidence affords no ground, even arguably, for allowing an appeal against conviction."

He moved on to comment on the sentence, saying: "So far as sentence is concerned, Ms Arshad, in written and oral submissions, submits that the imposition of a custodial sentence was wrong in principle because of the background to the offences which we have shortly summarised and the strong personal mitigation of the appellant: that we shall rehearse in a little detail in a moment. As we have already said, she is of previous good character and is now 48 years of age.

"The principal offence of which the appellant was convicted was possession of a firearm with intent to cause a belief that unlawful violence would be used, contrary to section 16A of the Firearms Act 1968. That offence is punishable with up to 10 years' imprisonment. An air pistol is a firearm for the purposes of the Act, and it is capable of causing serious injury or, in certain circumstances as this Court knows, death.

"The premeditated, deliberate discharge of a firearm in a public place, at least twice, having earlier tested the gun to make sure it was working, should, on the face of it, attract a custodial sentence of considerable length. If the courts were generally to respond to such conduct in any other way, it would be a recipe for both anarchy and injury of the innocent. As Lord Bingham of Cornhill Chief Justice said in Avis at page 185 to 186, referring to the Firearms Act 1968:

"Save for minor infringements which may be and are properly dealt with summarily, offences against these provisions will almost inevitably merit terms of custody, even on a plea of guilty, and in the case of an offender with no previous record. Where there are breaches of section 16A ... the custodial term is likely to be of considerable length."

"It is to be noted that Lord Bingham used the words 'almost inevitably' and 'likely to be'. He was not enunciating a principle of universal application. Everyone who is acquainted, however briefly, with what happens in our criminal courts knows that there are, from time to time, exceptional cases calling, if justice is to be done, for the delicate exercise of an often difficult discretion; albeit that, in recent times, Parliament, in its enthusiasm for mandatory minimum sentences and apparent determination to reduce judicial discretion, has seemed unwilling or reluctant to recognize this." This was a very opportune moment for the judiciary to express their displeasure at mandatory minimum sentences which threaten their autonomy.

Lord Justice Rose continued: "In the present case the sentencing exercise was extremely difficult. The Recorder cannot sensibly be criticised for heeding this Court's generally severe approach to the possession and use of firearms. The question which arises on this appeal is whether the circumstances were so exceptional that 6 months is manifestly excessive because either a non-custodial penalty, or a much shorter period of custody, was called for.

"The mitigation is great. The appellant, as we have said, is 48 years of age, with a family. She was of good character, not only in the sense that she had no previous convictions, but also because, as a teacher for 25 years, she had made a valuable and important contribution to the community in which she lived. She and her family, over a period of several months, had suffered the attacks on their home to which earlier we referred. The appellant believed that the incidents were linked and intended as harassment by youths in the neighbourhood. She also believed, on this eventful night that —— (PW1) was one of those responsible. Such harassment, even if —— (PW1) was responsible, may explain, though it does not begin to justify, the use of a firearm in the way we have described, particularly, when it was to be expected that the police were on their way to the scene. Old and recent history teaches us that those who take the law into their own hands are often unreliable when seeking to identify those whom they believe are properly the subject of their wrath.

"Additionally, however, the appellant was in a fragile mental state by reason, partly, of pressure at work, where for 3 years she had been working with emotionally disturbed children, with behavioural problems, and her school had recently been placed under Special Measures. Also, by reason of her age, she was undergoing mood swings and emotional upset. In consequence, she was suffering, in the terms of the psychiatrist's report, which was before the Recorder 'an adjustment disorder', making her more likely to overreact to minor stress. This may properly be regarded as reducing her culpability, though she was well aware of the consequences of her actions. She told the psychiatrist that her behaviour at the time of the offence had not been 'particularly sensible'.

"The pre-sentence report assessed the risk of re-offending and harm to the public as low and suggested a community punishment order. It also suggested, presciently in the light of subsequent events, that 'a custodial sentence could have the effect of making her a martyr to the media and those members of the public who feel anti-social behaviour is being dealt with too leniently'. There are, as is to be expected, excellent prison reports on the appellant."

The arguments put forward in my barrister's appeal document relating to the mitigation had been so convincing that Lord Justice Rose had actually included a lot of her words here. Despite that the governor at Styal prison and the police had not found my circumstances sufficiently exceptional to allow my HDC request!

He continued: "Taking all these features into account, it would, in our judgment, have been open to the Recorder to take the very exceptional course of imposing a non-custodial penalty. Even if custody were thought to be inevitable, a sentence of 3 months would have been just as effective as 6 months (see R v Ollerenshaw [1999] 1 Cr App R(S) 65). In any event, no useful public interest would now be served by the appellant's continued incarceration. We do not think, in the light of all the circumstances, that it is, at this stage, appropriate to impose a community penalty. Accordingly, we allow this appeal by quashing the sentence of six months and substituting a conditional discharge for 12 months."

After this, he turned to me and, as the law directs in the case of a conditional discharge, he explained the verdict in plain English to ensure that I fully understood.

"Mrs Walker, would you stand up a moment? What that means is simply this: that if, as I am sure will be the case, you do not get into any further trouble in the course of the next 12 months, you will hear no more about this. If you do commit any criminal offences, you can be brought back to court and re-sentenced for this offence. I am sure that will not happen. The order of the Court is a conditional discharge for 12 months, which I am sure you understand."

I later discovered that Donna had started receiving text messages, on silent, from friends congratulating us on my release even before Lord Justice Rose had finished speaking. Reporters dashed out to waiting cameras outside and the news of my release was instantly broadcast across the country. As I sat there in the dock, still surrounded by metal bars I was oblivious to the reaction that was going on outside.

I was about to find out for myself just how much interest my case had generated. The updates I had received from my family and my friends, the 'Free Linda' campaigners, had prepared me for this to a degree. However, I was amazed to find that to some extent, I had become famous on a national level.

32   Euphoric Release

Sitting in my cell, I had sometimes day-dreamed about what my early release would be like. I imagined that the Judge would announce that I was free to go and I would be able to leave the dock and walk out of the courtroom. Then, I would walk out onto the steps to have my photograph taken and thank my supporters. Instead, I was taken back down below. I would have to wait for release papers to come through from the prison. Sue Ann and my barrister came to congratulate me and I thanked them for their hard work. My barrister told me she had some experience of employment law and that in her opinion the judge had given me the conditional discharge to help me with my job. I was not aware of exactly what she meant by that at that time. They said that John, Donna, Craig and my dad were waiting and I asked them to send them away to get some lunch as it would be at least an hour before my release papers came through. Donna later told me that she and Craig had been chased by paparazzi photographing them as they crossed the road to find a café. My other son James had not come to London. He did not like all the fuss and publicity, unlike his twin Craig. I asked if I could use a phone to ring James. There were no public phones but a young lady guard told me to go to the toilet and I could use her mobile. Everyone was so excited for me. It was an incredible feeling. When I told James that I was being released, he said: "What, they're releasing you to wreak havoc on the streets again?" I could tell he was excited.

About an hour and a half later, I was taken to an office to be formally released. Here I was given a £45 release grant. I found this strange and told the guard that I was not homeless but apparently everyone receives this so I accepted it. I thought "this will buy 20 Smirnoff Ices for me and the girls when we get together to celebrate." I was then led down a corridor and released into the grand foyer. There, my family were waiting. They all looked gorgeous and very smart. I gave them all a hug. Then I noticed that Craig was wearing trainers with his smart shirt and trousers. "Where are your shoes?" I asked. "I forgot them," he said. Things were back to normal already, with me fussing over my family. They told me that the number of reporters outside was amazing and that I had to brace myself. All I could think was that I hadn't even been able to do my hair. I had managed to borrow a bit of lipstick and mascara from Sue Ann and my barrister but that was all. I thought: "My most famous moment and I look an awful sight!" I was quite confident about what I was going to say, however. I had it all written down. I had prepared for this moment and was going to enjoy it.

John clasped my hand and we walked out of the dimly lit grandeur of the Royal Courts of Justice into the streaming spring sunshine and a sea of cameras. The clicking was incessant and the journalists were jostling and trying to get their microphones well placed. They were each shouting my name and asking me to talk to them. I began to speak but had to start again as I was being jostled and shouted to. This is what I said.

"I am very happy to be going home. Thank you to everyone who has supported us through this ordeal and for the kindness we have been shown. "Special thanks to the 'Free Linda' campaigners. All the people who have written and sent cards, signed the petition, written to the papers and politicians, voted in the phone polls, spoken on the radio, TV and internet.

"Thank you to the British public!"

I had to stop for a moment to compose myself as I became overcome with emotion but I meant every word most sincerely. What I did not realise was that the programmes on radio and television were interrupted for it to be 'news flashed' across the country. I later discovered that perfect strangers as well as my own family and friends were cheering for me and jumping around at the news.

I think Tony Blair and the government had found my case to be an embarrassment. The opposition had certainly enjoyed using it as such. It was quite convenient for the government that my appeal fell the day prior to the general election and due to the overwhelming public interest in my case my release news flashed across the country. A cynical person may even think this was a damage limitation exercise – I wasn't complaining. People have told me they could remember where they were when they heard the news that I was being released, which I found quite astounding. Like when president Kennedy was shot. At the college where I used to work, one of my ex colleagues Wendy had run around the classrooms shouting to everyone: "Linda's out!"

Two cars were waiting for us at the front of the court. We had to fight a surge of photographers and then we could hardly open the doors to get in. I got into one with Donna and John. My dad and Craig followed in the other car. I waved as we left and Donna started to laugh.

"What are you waving for? Who do you think you are, the Queen?" she said.

We had a good giggle about that. The car took us back to the hotel where the family had stayed. There we transferred into the cars of two newspaper reporters called Keith Beabey and Bernard Ginns. John had been approached by a number of newspapers who wanted exclusive rights to my story.

We were to be paid a significant sum of money for the story which we felt considering the insecurity of my job we would have been foolish to refuse. So it was vital to them that the exclusivity of the story should be protected. They wanted to keep me away from other reporters for fear that they would glean some information from one of us, we were 'hot property' so we could not stop until we got out of London. I was not concerned about this affecting my fight for my job because they only wanted to write about my time in prison and they were a respectable paper so I knew the story would be accurate, unlike what had been claimed in the News of the World a few weeks earlier when it carried the headline, "I'd do it again"!

The car was a very comfortable Mercedes and it was lovely to sit and chat with John and Donna at last. I could look out through the window and watch the countryside fly by instead of squinting to see through a tiny tinted window from a closed box. I was back in society again, part of the community and part of my family once more. Donna kept receiving text messages congratulating us. As we drew nearer to home, my friend Sue rang on John's mobile. She had just called at our house on her way home from work in case we were back. Our road was full of press. She was unable to park her car and news crews were setting up lights in case we arrived home in the dark. I decided to repeat what I had said outside the appeal court, to thank everyone for their support and say how happy I was to be home with my family. Donna used her makeup to try to make me look a little more presentable for the cameras.

When we arrived home James had decorated the house with balloons and 'Welcome Home' banners and he and his girlfriend had bought me a bouquet of flowers and baked a chocolate flapjack for me. I gave him a hug and he felt like skin and bones, even thinner than before I went into prison. The phone was ringing constantly and we had to put the answer phone on, making a note of numbers and names to ring back later. We picked up the odd call if it was someone close. I shouted: "Hi it's me, I'm home!" It gave me an incredible buzz to say it. I enjoyed my first proper cup of tea with fresh milk. Donna's finance Rob and his mum were there as was Craig's partner Paul and their dog, Lucy. I gave Rob some of my release grant and he went out to buy some takeaway food for all of us. It tasted fantastic after the prison food.

Gradually, the excitement started to die down as people went home and left us to settle down. The phone was still ringing constantly. We turned on the television and watched ourselves on the news. Donna had kept all the news clippings in a folder for me and I was astounded to see how many there were. Every paper seemed to have covered the story, from nationals to the locals. Many of the papers had used photographs of the two youths and asked how this could be justice. The Daily Mirror had run a headline: "Call this Justice? Admired teacher driven to fire air pistol at yobs is jailed". The Daily Mail ran an article quoting Craig under the headline: "Why did police ignore 15 pleas by my mother to tackle the yobs?" He appeared in quite a few papers and I was very proud of him. The Sun wrote: "Justice Gone Mad" and the Sunday Times declared: "Linda Walker has paid a high price for tackling anarchy on her doorstep."

In the lounge and conservatory, the tables were piled high

with letters from well-wishers and every surface in the house was covered with cards. The letters were too numerous to summarise but I did eventually read each one and they were amazing. One woman from Liverpool wrote: "I drove to Manchester to sign your petition." I received a couple of lovely bouquets that day; one from Richard and Judy and one from GMTV. Both wanted me to appear on television the next morning. I had dozens of offers but decided I was not going to do anything as I did not want to jeopardize the hearing for my job and besides I was under contract to The Mail on Sunday. I was thoroughly interviewed by the reporters and the article appeared in the newspaper that Sunday; a big spread with a photograph of John and me under the headline: "They Crucified Me". All the other papers had also printed news of my release. The Daily Express said: "Teacher Who Tackled Yobs Freed: But why was she jailed in the first place?"

Sleeping in a proper bed that first night was such a luxury. The next day, I coloured my hair at last and felt a lot better. I also arranged for bouquets for all the 'Free Linda' campaigners, who had done such an amazing job. It stayed hectic at home for the first few days. The phone was ringing all the time and the press camped outside for three days. We kept up to date with the news cuttings and received more letters. I sent letters and made phone calls to thank people for their support. We also had a lot of celebrating to organise.

I arranged to take the girls out for an Italian meal and we went on holiday to the caravan with the family. Simple pleasures like food and being with the people I loved were even more wonderful after all that we had been through. We needed time to adjust and for everything that had happened to sink in. Even though the fight for my release was over and I was free from prison, I had learned a lot about the system and the law and was determined to fight to challenge the convictions. But first there was the fight for my career to pursue and the Police Complaints for myself and John to compile.

Some people assumed I would now just put everything that had happened behind me and simply get on with my life. I was looking forward to getting my life back to normal but I knew I could not move on until I had got some answers. As I had said to Sue Ann, "He may do it to someone else." At that point I believed the investigating DS had done something very wrong to us. But that view was naïve I now know it is much worse than that.

Whatever was going to become of me, if I was going to achieve any satisfaction regarding my grievances or not I knew one thing for sure; whatever I do wherever I go and whoever I am in the company of, the memory of being in prison will never be far from my mind. The utter futile frustration of being incarcerated, isolated, removed from my life. The agony of separation from those I love and the pain of those who love me. The boredom, the waste of precious time, the removal of free will is engraved in my consciousness forever. Life after prison is lived at a heightened state of awareness, with more appreciation of simple things that enrich a day, an hour, a minute. The relief of being out, of being free, is almost worth the incarceration. But I was one of the lucky ones I still had a life to come out to. Some people in prison loose everything and deservedly so you may say.

But not in every case!

PART 4

Post-Conviction Issues

33   Three and a Half Years Later

Three and a half years after the incident, on Tuesday 5th February 2008 I attended the General Teaching Council (GTC) in Birmingham for the hearing that would consider my fitness to remain a teacher. The GTC could effectively bar me from teaching by removing my teaching registration. The hearing had originally been scheduled for 18th October 2007 when we had been in Birmingham for a 9.30 start at the GTC headquarters. We had got up at 5 o'clock in the morning so we would not be late. I picked up my friend Sue, who had been a character referee for me at the trial, from her house in Mobberley whilst John went for Nigel my ex-head teacher who lived near Chester. He also had kindly agreed to come to be a professional character referee for me. We then met up near the M6 and travelled down together. My ex-boss Kath from college had also wanted to come, but I did not feel I could allow her to make the 400 mile round trip from Cumbria and back on her own on my behalf. It would have been too much of an imposition, so she provided a written character reference for me which stated that if I were to have my teaching registration removed, 'it would be a sad loss to teaching.' The principal from the college where I now teach two night classes had also prepared a written reference for me in which he stated that 'the college were happy to re-employ me.' Cliff Anderson my union representative had gone on the train from Preston.

We hit traffic near Birmingham so despite our early start we ended up on the last minute. When I arrived at the imposing Victorian red brick building in Victoria Square, Cliff and the barrister for the GTC were in conference so I waited in the small room that had been allocated to us. It was very civilized, water, coffee, tea and biscuits were available for us. When Cliff came out he was very flustered, he said the barrister intended to use as her opening 'statement of fact' to the hearing the sentencing remarks made by Recorder Browne in his judgement when I was sent to prison and to rely on them as a truthful account of what had happened on the night of the incident. I was very disturbed at this decision because Recorder Browne had stated, "You were, as you conceded, ranting and raving like a lunatic. These boys denied any involvement in any of the anti-social acts committed against you and there is no evidence whatsoever that would contradict those denials." That evidence is now available. "You approached PW 1 and fired at least two pellets from the pistol at the ground near to his feet." and "there can be no excuse whatsoever for what you did that night. Even had those *children* been involved in anti-social activity against you"

I said that I could not agree to this as an 'agreed statement of facts' because it did not fairly represent the circumstances of the incident. Cliff was anxious to proceed with the hearing. John and my witnesses had all taken the day off work and got up at the crack of dawn to attend this hearing. Cliff said what was important was the mitigation and the sooner we got to that the better. I felt under pressure to agree to the judgement as a fair summary of the facts. Even John was saying, 'come on

Linda lets get it over with.' He had had enough of all the years this case had taken and how it had ruled our lives. I couldn't help but feel if such a prejudicial account was initially presented to the panel my character would be so badly damaged in their eyes that it would be beyond redemption and impossible to retrieve. I had been here before at the trial! So I adamantly said it was not right and that I could not agree to it. I had spent the last three years of my life fighting the untruths which it contained. Sue grasped the full implications of the situation and said, "How can she agree?" Nigel didn't comment. Cliff said it would look bad if the hearing could not proceed when everyone had travelled from far and wide and the panel had stayed in Birmingham last night to be here. He said it may go against me when they considered what sanction to impose against me. John was worried about this also and kept urging me to agree but I couldn't. I said, "I may as well have just got a job, any job, and not spent the last three years of my life writing letters to correct untruths, sitting up until 3 a.m. in the morning sometimes, on the computer and not being able to go to bed because I was obsessed with obtaining fairness." I turned on my John and said, "and what's the matter with you? Why have you lost your bottle all of a sudden?" We hadn't capitulated all the way along when they wanted me to plead guilty to a lesser charge and drop the charges against John so why should I now go against what I believed was right? I felt John was betraying me although I understood he had had enough and he was worried for me but I knew he would support me whatever I decided because he always does, he is my rock. Cliff went back in to talk with the barrister.

It was really tense. I had not been prepared for this level of pressure, I had understood that it would not be an adversarial process but it did not feel like that. I asked "Why was what I did and what I fully admitted not enough? "Why does it have to be exaggerated and made to sound worse? "I admitted everything that I did, why can't they be satisfied with that?" I could not understand why the barrister for the GTC would want to exaggerate the incident, but apparently it was her job. I suppose it was because the convictions were so very serious, but because of the conditional discharge the convictions could not be used against me, so the case for the GTC had to reflect the seriousness of those convictions. When Cliff came out he said, "We are going for a postponement!" This would allow us to provide the evidence from GMP which established that it was never proved that the air pistol was loaded, which seemed to be the main bone of contention. So everyone had had a wasted trip and I worried that my character referees may not be able to make it next time.

Over an hour after the scheduled time that it was supposed to commence we entered the hearing and sat before the panel, the three people who would decide what sanction, if any, to impose upon me, the offending teacher. The two teacher and one lay person members all looked rather put out and wooden at being kept waiting. The two reporters who were sat in the public seats looked bemused. Cliff spoke to ask for a postponement to allow evidence to be presented that would challenge one part of the allegation against me, the part that stated that I had fired pellets. The allegation was one of professional misconduct, conduct not compatible with the professional standards expected of a registered teacher, which I had fully admitted that I had committed by my actions. The barrister for the GTC then spoke and was rather derogatory about us blaming us for the delay in not being prepared for the hearing, which I did not really think was very fair as it was she who had departed from the agreed statement of facts to the judgement of Recorder Browne on the actual morning of the hearing. The panel did not object to the postponement so it was agreed that we would be back at a later date. Next time I would bring everything with me, all the documents relating to the case including the court transcripts of the trial. I did not intend to be short of any evidence that may be required next time.

The press were intrigued and asked Cliff what the new evidence was and did it prove I wasn't guilty? I felt I had lived to fight another day, but I knew once again I had a fight on my hands. If I wanted to keep my freedom to teach, which I desperately did to retrieve some shred of dignity, I would alongside Cliff, have to fight for it.

The fight for my job had entailed a disciplinary hearing which had resulted in my dismissal for gross misconduct, twelve days after I was released from prison. I had made the front page with Posh and Beck's in the *Daily Mail* on Tuesday 17th May with the headline "NOW THE JAILED TEACHER IS SACKED" and was again overwhelmed by the support of the public. Phone polls on Granada Reports came out at 96% that I should not have been sacked, and I received many more letters and cards. One of the letters I received was from a barrister Dr. Jennifer Coleman, who alerted me to the fact that my dismissal may be invalid for the reason of my sentence being reduced to a 'conditional discharge'. She informed me that conditional discharges do not count for purposes of disciplinary proceedings and that being the case I had been dismissed unlawfully and unfairly. She sent the letter to me by 'special delivery' for which I was most grateful. She said she hated injustice and 'kangaroo courts' run by people who did not know or care about the law and reacted in a 'knee jerk' fashion. Other letters and a telephone call received had also indicated the same. A man from Bolton had spent all afternoon in the library researching the law on my behalf!

As it turned out they were right. Legislation contained in the Powers of Criminal Courts (sentencing) Act 2000 states: "An absolute or conditional discharge should be deemed not to be a conviction for any other purpose other than the purposes of the proceedings in which the order is made." So categorically this was the case. An appeal hearing followed at which my dismissal was upheld. Councillor Mann for Salford City Council, lead person for education released a statement on behalf of Salford Education Authority. He said: "Clearly the school and Local Education Authority must make their first consideration the safety of the children in their care. I have no doubt that Mrs. Walker felt under considerable pressure at the time of her offence some might say her reaction is understandable, but it is certainly not acceptable in a country which rightly prides itself on the rule of law and its consistent application." I was annoyed at the implication that I was a danger to children and also thought how misguided he was to talk about this country's pride in the law after my recent experience.

This was followed by my case for unfair dismissal going to the Employment Tribunal (ET) in January 2006. A damning statement was delivered by the head teacher who did not want me back under any circumstances. She said the school had appointed staff to cover my timetable. My other duties had been delegated between other staff including the 'two' new deputy heads! Salford had told her she would not be insured if she chose to employ me due to new policies introduced. So they had effectively forbidden her to employ me. Also she alleged, even after reading my character references and though she does not know me (her appointment was not until after my suspension) she could not employ a person who is as 'equally unpredictable' as the children at school. Bearing in mind that the school is a 'Special School' for children with 'Social Emotional and Behavioural Difficulties' and some of those children are extremely disturbed, it was a very serious insult and accusation. They were by now well aware that they could not use the convictions against me and insisted that they had relied upon the facts of my actions, but even at this stage in the proceedings the head teacher continued to claim that I had shot at people, still relying upon the inaccurate report from the police.

Although it was found by the ET that my employers had acted unreasonably in not allowing me to contribute to their investigation via an interview to which I was contractually entitled, overall my dismissal was upheld as a reasonable response. I was deeply upset at losing my job. When I got home I felt like I had been punched! Yobbery had won! The television cameras and photographers had followed me down the road, clicking, to sell their pictures. The phone was ringing with newspapers wanting quotes, all earning a living from me and I had no job. I had never had the sack before. I didn't want to get another job and have to contend with people's suspicions about me. I wanted my job, where my pupils and their parents knew me and trusted me and knew I would never have threatened violence to a young person. When the day after I spoke to Cliff he said, "They definitely did consider the conviction Linda it ran through the whole of their case," but they had said they hadn't, that they had only considered my actions. "But we can't prove it Linda, proving it is another matter." The union declined to pursue my case for unfair dismissal further.

My conduct was also under investigation by the Department for Education and Skills (DfES) as it was then, now the Department for Children Schools and Families, as a child protection issue. This meant I could be barred from working with children altogether by being placed on list 99 if they found I posed a risk to children. This sanction although mainly reserved for paedophiles was a possibility in my case. I had been invited to submit evidence for my defence. A report had been sent from an Assistant Chief Constable (ACC) of GMP to the DfES. That report omitted everything that was incriminating to the witnesses; it did not mention the chanting and fronting up to me and stated there was no evidence to connect the youths to the car on the drive. It also stated that we 'allege' that we have been repeated victims of vandalism as if it were untrue, that I showed "no remorse whatsoever" and I had stated, "it was my full intention to put the victims in fear." Finally it stated, "Mrs Walker informed the officers she was going through the menopause which was affecting her nerves and causing her to be on edge." As if my actions had nothing whatsoever to do with the crime and vandalism against my home and family! Following my arrest I had made the police officers laugh, when I was asked for my date of birth I had said as I gave it, "Yes I am a menopausal maniac!" It was my prerogative to joke about this myself but for him to use it against me was blatant sexual discrimination. I had not been provided with a copy of this report despite two subject access requests, one prior to my going to prison and one after. I was entitled to see it under the Data Protection Act.

34   All Talk No Action

On Saturday 3rd June 06, one year and eight months after it was lodged, the police complaint report had hit the wooden floor in the hall with a thud. It sounded like a telephone book had been delivered. The investigating DS had responded to our complaints via a written report which he had compiled with the assistance of his solicitor, this had taken him three months to compile. The 52 page police complaint report contained some 147 points written in paragraphs.

At the section on background information the substantial history of vandalism and crime at our house since May 2002, when our fish were first stolen from the pond is acknowledged. The report states regarding crimes that were undetected, one in 2002 and three in 2004, that 'none had evident lines of enquiry,' although they had not attended in relation to any of these incidents. It cited this may help to explain the frustration stress and anxiety that John and I say we suffered during the two years prior to the incident. It noted that I declined to give a statement regarding that I witnessed PW 1 and his associate place a road sign into the road. Why was it not taken at the time when it would have supported my claims about the youths? Or have I just answered my own question?

It was acknowledged it was relevant that John and I believed we had a serious ongoing problem with persons affecting our quality of life, it also stated that we were unaware of who the perpetrators were. It stated, "If the names of the youths they now suspect had been offered, namely PW 1 and his associates <u>this would have resulted in them being questioned and if any evidence were revealed, warned by the police for harassment</u> prior to the firearms incident." This is what I thought would happen when the identity of the youths became known to the police on the 14th August 2004.

Regarding our allegation of perjury against PW 1 it reported that although the investigating DS deliberately did not take the statements from Mr. Matthews (our milkman) to remain impartial to defence allegations of influencing the witness. He did conduct the enquiry and the advice file submitted, the case for the perjury allegation to the CPS, was provided by him. When the senior CPS prosecutor received the file it contained both statements of David Mathews (our milkman). This meant that she had not received it until after the 9th March 2004 when the second one was written, after my application to appeal was lodged. My application had almost not gone in awaiting this decision. The report discloses that PW 1 was *never interviewed* regarding the allegation. It also disclosed the advice file did not mention the criminal culpability of PW 1 and his associate with regard to the placing of a road sign to endanger life. It confirmed that the perjury prosecution was not pursued due to 'insufficient evidence,' even though it is accepted that possible lines inquiry were not pursued by the DS or suggested by the CPS!

I had complained that my appeal had effectively been sabotaged by the police casting doubts upon Mr. Matthews (milkman) statements to the police. The new evidence if put to the jury would have proved PW 1 was untruthful in the evidence he gave on oath. The report concluded that the evidence of PW 1 was not crucial to my conviction stating that, "it was Linda Walker's own actions as admitted in interview and court that led to her conviction." Regarding the description which I had complained did not fit the circumstances, "the defendant Linda Walker approached local youths in the street after midnight with a ***shotgun*** and a ***handgun*** screaming at them. She discharged the gun and ***shot 5 or 6 bullets at the feet of the youths.***" The investigating DS stated he did not have any knowledge of this document! Administrative staff do not undertake investigation, they only have access to information that is provided to them by police officers. It was found, "there is no evidence that any police officer had any responsibility for this document as such." It was disclosed however that the DS presented his case to the CPS in person and had provided a verbal account of our interviews.

The evidence surely was provided by the document itself.

Regarding TV and radio broadcasts the investigating DS denied any intention to mislead by his portrayal of the incident: by presenting the weapons, rifle cocked up and pistol with gas canisters and pellets in the case, also by his claim that I 'found' some local youths on a nearby street some 500 yards away from my home. Regarding that I was classified as a POOPP (priority prisoner) at HMP Buckley Hall and I had been informed it was a status set by the arresting force GMP the report concluded "no evidence was found to suggest that any officer of GMP had submitted a report to the prison service that had any adverse affect on her or the conditions of her imprisonment." So how I came to be classified as such was still a mystery. Perhaps that too had been a verbal account, possibly a telephone call? I was beginning to think that 'no evidence was found,' was police speak for, 'it didn't happen,' only it did!

In respect of the report that was prepared by the Chief Inspector for the disciplinary hearing at which I was dismissed, the police complaint report stated that it was based on the investigation of the DS and that it reflected the *'crown's stance in court'* or the *'prosecution's position'.*

It admitted 'minor inaccuracies' in the report to my employers;

The trespass and taking of a gallon container of unknown liquid from a private garden and pouring it over a car at the same private property is an act of the vandalism.

It was concluded this was my, "personal interpretation."

On the issue of whether I had stated to the youths I was going to shoot them the CI said I had said this in the 999 call and that it was, "a matter of semantics."

Regarding that his report stated I shot "at the feet" of one of the youths when I shot at the tarmac the CI responded that this was, "a matter of speech." I did offer to demonstrate the difference.

Regarding the strong inferences that I was drunk contained within the report it was concluded that CI's statement, "was inaccurate and did not reflect Linda Walker's physical condition as recorded on the custody record on arrival at the station." This error was attributed to, "a genuine misunderstanding" on his part.

Regarding his claim that I had, 'elected for trial by jury' which I objected to because it inferred I had chosen the high profile trial which my employers claimed had brought the school into disrepute. This again it was reported as, "an error on his part."

Regarding his claim, "she did shoot the pistol at them" this was described as, "a reasonable interpretation of events."

The incorrect length of my original prison sentence was accepted as a "genuine factual error."

Regarding the opinion which inferred I should have got more than five years he stated that he was asked for his opinion and he is entitled to it.

The comments, "Lack of integrity" and, "Manipulation of the media" were also accepted as expressions of his opinions.

The mistake regarding the distance the youths were from our house was once again dismissed as, "a simple use of English" issue.

Chief Inspector Mathews, assisted by Inspector McCulloch who had undertaken the investigation of my police complaint, concluded there were a number of factual inaccuracies in the report prepared by the CI that could have been avoided if greater care had been taken by the report writer, however it was found,

"CI —— did not intentionally mislead or tell blatant lies as alleged."

No formal sanction was recommended. Putting it down to mistakes was the least damaging scenario for the police. It did say that my claiming the report from the police was flawed had put GMP in a bad light following my Employment Tribunal. Well their 'factually inaccurate' report hadn't done a lot for my career either!

Surely now it was admitted this was the 'crowns stance in court' or 'the prosecutions position,' this was an admission that the case against us in court was wrong and based on false premise?

At the conclusion of the report the evidence that had been ignored and dismissed was acknowledged, it stated it was understandable that Linda Walker and John Cavanagh had concerns regarding PW 1 and his associates and cited our reasons:-

"Two burglars who had burgled Linda Walker's shed in July 2003 were known associates of both police witnesses.

The history with Mrs. Walker's sons

The incident reported by the milkman

The road sign incident witnessed by Mrs. Walker

Their admitted vicinity to her house when the plastic gallon container was placed on the car"

Despite these findings and conclusions no evidence of bias or impropriety was found against the investigating DS. This I found perplexing given the numerous admissions and disclosures in the report and the issues that remained unexplained.

The senior IPCC commissioner who had supervised the police complaint investigation was Ms Nazeem Malik.

We were informed when the police complaint report was received that if we wished to appeal we had 28 days in which to do so. The report had arrived three weeks to the day before the wedding of my daughter Donna to Rob. The 'World Cup' theme wedding was to be a neutral celebration for the pair of opposing football fans, the bride a born and bred junior blue and now fully fledged Manchester City fan whilst the groom a red blooded Man. United supporter. I was doing the catering, a carvery buffet for 70 guests in the day and a finger buffet for 100 at night. I had wanted to do it anyway but now it was more a necessity than an option if they were to have the wedding reception I wanted, but could not really now afford. I had a lot of shopping and preparation to do but first I wanted to make sure that our appeals went in. It was a very busy time for me but as I was not actually in any paid employment people seemed to think I had all the time in the world. Whilst I had been waiting for the police complaint report I had also kept busy doing a lot of decorating in the house. Craig had helped me to decorate our dining kitchen, the hall stairs and landing and mine and John's bedroom and en suite bathroom. This had been a few good weeks work and was in preparation for the house going up for sale now that I had lost my job.

35   Just Too Serious!

I had decided to pursue an appeal, against my dismissal from my job, myself to the Employment Appeal Tribunal (EAT). On the 7th July 2006 I finished all the pots and the laundry from the wedding, and then I submitted my skeleton argument for the preliminary hearing at the EAT. My case cited:

"The respondent's case relied on that the convictions are proof enough of serious misconduct on the part of the claimant and adequately reflect her actions. The claimant asserts that the conditional discharge is a reflection of her actions and the considerable mitigation." My case relied upon that that my ex-employers had relied upon my convictions and this was unlawful. I booked the train tickets to London and made a reservation at the Travel Lodge on Drury Lane, where John, Donna, Craig and my dad had stayed when they came to fetch me home. It cost money we could ill afford, but I had no time to work I was too busy fighting for my job back. I couldn't move on until I had convinced myself I had fought as hard as I could and done everything in my power to get it back.

Going to the EAT in London reminded John of when he had been here the year before and had carried the box with my petition, the ten thousand plus signatures of my guardian angels, to the Royal Courts of Justice. The court building was a grand old Georgian house. It was on the embankment overlooking the River Thames. Lots of landmark places were in view. We could see the dome of Saint Paul's cathedral and to the right London Bridge. Down the river we could just about see the Houses of Parliament, the London Eye which we had been told not to miss dominated the horizon. We had not been on it, we are both afraid of heights and were not interested in jollying anyway I was here on a mission. My legal skills may not be up to much but I was going to do my best. I thought "I am a teacher, what I am good at is a communicating."

In court I could see as I got part way through that the judge was not accepting my arguments. He started huffing and puffing, at one point he said to me, "What did you expect?" I told him that 'factual inaccuracies' in the report to school about me had been upheld by the Police Complaint investigation and that I had the proof with me, the report. He agreed to look at it and adjourned for this purpose. The report had not upheld one single aspect of my complaint; every allegation had been dismissed as 'unsubstantiated.' Even the factual inaccuracies which were admitted were put down to, 'non-intentional mistakes' and, "a matter of speech" they were, "not deliberate." So my allegation regarding these mistakes being 'lies' was unsubstantiated also.

When the judge returned from his adjournment he commented on the complaint being 'mainly unsubstantiated.'

Apparently in law, the employer only has to show that they have 'reasonable grounds' to suspect that I committed the misconduct in question. Whether I did or not, not the question here, but did they have reasonable grounds to suspect that I did? The police report and the serious convictions provided the reasonable grounds for them to suspect I did commit the misconduct in question. I knew I had committed misconduct but not of the gravity assumed by the convictions. The judge also referred to the seriousness of the charges which I could not contend so in the end it proved to be futile. The convictions were again just too serious. The more I lost as I went along the more I lost credibility for my case. It didn't matter that the house of cards case was built on foundations of untruth, the house of cards still stood.

I could have carried on and appealed this decision but I could not see any point. If my best efforts had failed what more could I do? So I decided to call it the end of the road as far as my job was concerned. We came out at 12.30 p.m. Our train home was not until 4.40 p.m. so we got a taxi to Covent Garden and had Cornish pasties for lunch. John sat with the bags on the stone steps and watched the street entertainers whilst I went for mooch around the shops and market. I brought a dress in the sale at Monsoon. It was 70% off, a good bargain. I did not feel upset, not like the after the ET hearing. I had given it my best shot and that is all I had wanted to do. Beside that, my credit card was still operational. When I sorted all my papers though, I uncovered a 'schedule of losses' that Cliff had prepared for the Employment Tribunal which put my loss of salary (including pension contributions etc.) to 6th December 2006 at **£50,982.34p**. More than double what I had received from the paper.

Five weeks and one day later on 5th September 2006 GMP under the instruction of the IPPC wrote to Salford City Council to correct their factually inaccurate report. The Human Resources Department of City of Salford's Childrens Services received a letter from GMP informing them that following investigation the report that had been provided to them, "contained certain inaccuracies and opinions."

I was copied into the correspondence and my letter stated, "Please find enclosed a copy of the letter sent to Salford LEA regarding the inaccuracies in the investigatory meeting document." It was claimed this was, 'in fairness to Linda Walker' and 'to allow you to amend and maintain an accurate case record.' There was no mention of any apology for the wide range of the untruthful statements. The inaccuracies that were corrected included: *(in italics)* Referring to my firing the air pistol: *"At the at the feet of the boys"* that it was *"loaded"* and *"that she did fire the pistol at them"* The comment that inferred I was drunk, *"Given that that she had been drinking alcohol police were required to leave her for eight hours"* also *"Mrs Walker elected for the case to be heard at the Crown Court-trial by jury"* lastly *"Lack of integrity"* and *"Manipulation of the media."*

What was not rescinded was the whole out of context view of the incident that the report conveyed, the context which was now acknowledged in GMP's own police complaint report. The CI had said "had the situation been reversed and the youths had opened fire at her they would likely have received a custodial sentence of about five years" (I hadn't opened fire at them). This was incorrect as youths receive lighter sentences in regard to air weapon incidents in accordance with government guidelines which recommend 'consideration of cautions and warnings.' I would have thought he would have known that. It would have been much better if it had been re-written. The most incriminating parts of the report however <u>had</u> been rescinded.

Two weeks later we received the decisions regarding our Police Complaint Appeals from the IPCC, a senior commissioner stated in letters to us, "I do not consider the broader conclusions of the investigation were inappropriate. There is no evidence that GMP failed to consider relevant evidence or that their conclusions were unreasonable." There was one exception, my complaint against the Chief Inspector's report about which she stated,

"The risk to the force and the public of a senior officer who provides inaccurate information is substantial." I noticed the public didn't come first.

"I recommend that Chief Inspector —— receive a written warning with an undertaking that the force monitor or supervise his work to ensure that standards are met. In addition I recommend that the inaccuracies found are retracted in writing, although I believe this has now been done." So, the report to Salford had not been provided of the CI's or GMP's own volition, but only after they had been instructed to do so by the IPCC. I had requested this on numerous occasions but with no response.

In my response to the IPCC appeal reports I wrote, "It is unfortunate that your findings did not uncover more extensive misconduct but if as you state "my role is not to carry out independent investigation" then that was never a possibility." In that respect I find this process to be unsatisfactory." regarding the investigation of my police complaint. I wanted the source of the inaccurate information investigated. I wrote, "I do appreciate the significant efforts made on CI Mathews and Inspector McCullock's part in undertaking this extensive investigation on our behalf but feel they were unable to obtain sufficient evidence regarding our complaints due to non-cooperation of officers in closing ranks and guarding secrets.

How did I become classified as a 'Prolific Offender or Other Priority Prisoner' whilst in HMP Buckley Hall?

How did the CPS come to be in possession of such a biased

and vastly exaggerated to the point of untruthful version of events?

It is an unsolved mystery, someone knows and that it has not been revealed indicates a conspiracy."

The IPCC's letter of response fully supported the DS's investigation stating;

"Absolutely no misconduct or impropriety has been found on DS ——'s part." and "None of the inaccuracies found in the report were found to come from DS ——'s the findings of the investigation. They are all found to be genuine mistakes rather than evidence of malicious intent on CI —— part."

Also "DS ——'s conduct has not been found wanting."

I found these conclusions to be astonishing and wrote and told the Chief Constable of GMP Michael Todd so. I asked him, "If the investigation carried out by DS —— was so exemplary proper and correct, where have other officers repeatedly got their incorrect information from?" I appealed to him to re-open the investigation into my case. I cited that it was an issue of public protection. But GMP seemed very enthusiastic to support the DS's investigation which right at the onset, when details of my complaint were taken by Inspector Kath Booth she had told us, "If that is what happened then that is wrong."

GMP and the IPCC refused to correspond with me any further regarding the appeal of my police complaint report stating:

"Both GMP and the IPCC consider that this matter is now closed. We will not re-open or review this complaint any further." (An Assistant Chief Constable wrote for Chief Constable Todd.)

"GMP considers the matter closed and will not be entering into any further correspondence on the matter with you." (A Detective Superintendent of GMP Internal Affairs wrote.)

And finally,

"Please note I will not be responding to any further correspondence in relation to this complaint." (An IPCC commissioner wrote.)

I was distraught I had spent two years trying to get to the truth. I decided to write to my MP Bev Hughes. Her support had been so reassuring to me earlier. I thought, "If they won't answer me they will have to answer her." So I wrote and updated her of the developments in my case.

In October 2006 I was invited to attend an interview at the DfES in Darlington in the North East. Prior to attending the meeting I wrote to inform them about the corrections in the report of the CI to Salford LEA by GMP also of the impending likelihood of corrections in the report from the Assistant Chief Constable to them following that this matter was under investigation. I pointed out the extensive range of misinformation that had been conveyed to them. I hoped this would limit the damage from the said report which was obviously not a priority for GMP. It is quite disturbing that action to rectify misinformation on their part, only ever seems to take place after the damage was done!

At the interview Sir Roger Singleton (ex head of Dr Barnado's) asked how I would react if anything like this were to happen again. I told him that I had joked about that to my friends saying, "I would shoot them and then bury them under the shed!" This did make the point though that I did not have to have phoned the police and given them my name and address if my intention had been to commit serious crime. I then went on to say that seriously I would demand my rights and would insist that the police took action and not tolerate just being given a crime reference number over the phone after waiting twenty minutes for them to answer. I would complain most vigorously and demand action. He concluded, "You would be more assertive?" and I agreed saying, "Yes, I would not just politely accept them fobbing me off." I also made the point that it was not fair to consider me a danger to children when my actions had been aimed at protecting my own children from what I perceived was a threat to their safety. The interview ended after one and a half hours which Cliff seemed to think quite short.

A couple of weeks later I heard from Bev Hughes. She advised me of the possibility to pursue taking my case to the Criminal Case Review Commission (CCRC) who, if I had the grounds, could look again at my case with a view to possibly challenging my convictions; their function to investigate possible miscarriages of justice!

36   GMP Requested to Apologise

In my case to the CCRC I relied on that I did not get a fair trial, because the case presented against me was untruthful. A list of untruthful claims taken from the prosecutions opening and closing speeches was quoted and it filled two pages of A4 paper.

It was by this time over a year since I complained about the report that had been sent to the DfES about me from the ACC. The right to 'Confidentiality' is part of the Police Code of Conduct and includes that any information provided by them is accurate. Trying to get any satisfaction via these complaints was like trying to pull out my own teeth which I thought was probably a very effective strategy for them under normal circumstances. Anyone less determined or without the time and support which I had could not have continued, especially if they were paying for legal representation. I didn't have the income to do that but I did have the time and the support.

On Valentines Day 2007 I received the decision regarding the report from the ACC to the DfES. Ms Nazeem Malik, senior commissioner for the IPCC stated,

"The issue here is that the error's came from the source material of DS —— in both ACC —— and CI —— cases. As a supervising officer to DS —— it is CI —— who has received the formal advice and that is where the discipline sanctions should stop. It would not be reasonable to continue to sanction other officers for one officer's error. However, as the police have acknowledged that there were errors in the letter it may be worth considering apologising for the errors and rectifying them. I am aware the errors have been retracted in the case of CI —— and a corrected letter has been sent to the LEA informing them of the errors in the report. I see no reason why this should not also be done by GMP in a letter to the DfES." Finally it stated under, "ACTIONS REQUIRED OF THE FOFCE/AUTHORITY

"Request GMP to rectify the errors made in the letter to the DfES and consider apologising to Mrs. Walker for these errors."

Regarding the admission that the errors came from the investigating DS's source this contrasted starkly to the very supportive statements made regarding his investigation in our police complaint appeal reports!

The following day I received a letter from the DfES, their decision. The letter was dated 8th February 07 and stated, "Officials in the Department for Education and Skills acting for the Secretary of State have considered the information in this matter. It has been further examined by Sir Roger Singleton, supported by his panel of experts, who has provided advice to the Secretary of State. Taking into account that information, the considerations of those officials and the advice of Sir Roger Singleton, the Secretary of State has decided not to bar or restrict your employment." I was not barred from working with children. I was really thrilled about this decision and started to plan that maybe I could do some voluntary work, a cookery club with disabled children at a local special school in Trafford. I thought that this would be a bit of fun for the children and me also I hoped it may help me to re-build my reputation. It was not a 'let off' however as the letter stated, "you are warned that your behavior has caused great concern." And "as you are registered with the General Teaching Council of England, the matter will be referred to them for their consideration." Another battle to look forward to – not!

I can understand how GMP must have felt aggrieved at having to apologise to me after I that made that stupid phone call and I do appreciate I must take responsibility for my actions. Even after taking all of that into consideration though, my convictions are way over the top and I consider I have a lot more cause to feel aggrieved than them. I believe the actions of the DS and those who upheld his investigation undermine the credibility of the Police force and their profession much more than I did mine, but I wasn't acting in a professional capacity, and I was ill. He certainly caused a lot more damage and a massive waste of resources. The costs that were incurred in bringing the case against me could have been used to put away a proper criminal!

As Easter 2007 approached I sent a card to Bev Hughes. In it I informed her that I had submitted my case to the CCRC and thanked her for her advice on this matter. I also informed her of the decision by the Secretary of State that I had not been barred from working with children. I felt I owed her this courtesy. Also as she was now the Minister for Children I was proud to tell her, thinking it would a show her that she was right to assist me as she had. After Easter I received a lovely card from her with a handwritten personal message which said, "I was very pleased about the Secretary of State's decision recently – he made the right judgement." I was beginning to see some light at the end of my tunnel and felt I was at last on my way to finding some closure.

In June 2007 I received a letter from the Criminal Cases Review Commission which stated that my application had been considered and they had reached a provisional view that it should **not** be referred to appeal. A Provisional Statement of Reasons was provided to explain how this decision was reached. In the light of what was disclosed by the police complaint report and the corrections made in police reports I was quite shocked. I had felt quite confident I had sufficient grounds for my case to at least be considered for appeal and I wrote and told them so.

Later in June I received a final decision from the CCRC. It was <u>not</u> to refer my case and stated very abruptly "your case has now been closed." It enclosed a Final Statement of Reasons which adduced,

"Mrs. Walker is seeking to reopen the case on the basis that the police version of events was untrue. This was the defence case at trial and was rejected by the jury." But it was untrue! This did not now bode well for my upcoming hearing at the GTC. Fighting a conviction is a very difficult feat; it is a challenge against the establishment. Every conviction overturned is a crack in the foundations upon which the justice system stands. I think the establishment believed I would just be happy to be released. As a victim of crime and vandalism I am disgusted but as a victim of institutional discrimination I feel violated.

Whilst at our caravan in the summer holidays of 2007 I watched the news regarding the Jean Charles de Menezes police complaint report. The police had not been truthful about that incident either when he was shot seven times in the head on the London tube suspected of carrying a suicide bomb. The report was delivered live by senior IPCC commissioner, Nazeem Malik, who had managed the case. I thought it was quite a coincidence that she had also managed this high profile, and for the police, highly embarrassing case.

37   The General Teaching Council Hearing

Just before Christmas 2007 I challenged the decision of the CCRC at an application hearing for a judicial review. This was an oral hearing with two high court judges which was done by video link in Manchester to the Royal Courts of Justice, Court of Appeal in London. I politely presented my case arguing, how could my convictions be lawful when a prosecution witness, it was now accepted, had lied in court? Also, following safeguards put in place after the tragic case of Stephan Kishco regarding that evidence inconvenient to the prosecution can not be suppressed, I asserted that evidence relating to the air pistol not being loaded was suppressed by the prosecution's insistence that it was loaded, when evidence, that clearly indicated otherwise, was available.

Lord Justice Maurice Kay with Justice Stanley Burton explained to me that whether the decision was fair or not was not of concern in cases such as these. The pistol being loaded or not was irrelevant to the charge and the evidence relating to the youths had already been presented to the court of appeal and been judged as inadmissible. It was not new evidence so the case was dismissed. He did however deliver a new judgement and his statement was accurate. He had taken account of the full circumstances of the incident. So finally although the judgement still stood, at least the judgement was accurate and provided a more truthful record. This I thought would help my case at the GTC when we were to return on the 5th February 2008.

The date duly arrived and the barrister for the GTC was still determined to present the judgement of Recorder Browne as evidence, her case being it was still a valid high court judgement, because I had not been successful in challenging my convictions the judgement still stood. I was equally as insistent that I wanted the new judgement of Lord Justice Maurice Kay and Stanley Burton presented which I felt presented a much more accurate view and as I understood it, superseded the judgement of Recorder Browne. So it was copied and provided to the panel as an extra document to the bundle of documents.

Cliff was not in agreement with including more evidence that was as he saw it against me, but I wanted it in because even though it had refused me permission to challenge my convictions it acknowledged my actions in a truthful context. Because Cliff was not in agreement to its submission I had to tell the panel myself why I wanted to add this document to the bundle. I told them it was the third judgement in my case, and although it had refused me permission to seek a judicial review it had taken account of the mistakes and inaccuracies established via my police complaint, that were presented against me in earlier judgements. I told them the new judgement did not state that I fired pellets. It accepted that there was evidence available that indicated these were the youths who had been committing crime and vandalism against us, also it did not refer to the youths as 'children' as the youth in question was 18years and 10months old at the time of the incident. I was pleased I had been able to get this in right at the onset of the hearing which hopefully would deflect any damage that may be done by the presentation of the judgement of Recorder Browne.

There were now several quite long adjournments whilst the panel, which was a new panel, read the new documents that had been presented. We sat in our little room and drank coffee and ate biscuits. It seemed less tense this time. Two of the panel had declared an interest; a teacher member was the annually elected president of the union, my union and the lay chairperson declared that her husband was a member of the Association of Chief Police Officers, and was a firearms expert. We did not object because I thought we had one from each camp really, and it did not mean they were prejudice in any one direction personally. It was almost lunch time by the time we got started presenting the evidence.

I presented a prepared statement, my account of what had happened on the night. I then answered questions. I had to explain why I had told the Police the air pistol was loaded and how I now came to claim otherwise. I explained that it was an assumption based on my belief that it would not fire unless it was not loaded which was a mistake but I had not known this at the time. Cliff asked me to explain how the crime and vandalism against us had made me feel. I told them that it had made my life intolerable, that it had made John ill and that I was sick with worry for my boys. That it had affected the relationships within our family. I explained that we did not know who it was who was targeting us or why and because of that I did not know how far they were prepared to go. I was worried for the safety of my own children and perceived that they were under attack. Talking about it brought it all back to me and I did get upset thinking about John having physical pain and my boys being worried and frightened. I was later portrayed in the Manchester Evening News as weeping while I gave my evidence which was a bit of a dramatisation. I explained that I knew what I had done was wrong, that it was a terrible thing to do to take a weapon onto the street and I expressed my shame at my actions and said how sorry I was.

My witnesses were then called to give their evidence. They read their prepared statements and no questions were put to Sue or Nigel except to ask them for their present occupations; Sue is an administrative director for a private day nursery and school whilst Nigel is still a head teacher. Their professions gave them enormous credibility. John was questioned in quite an aggressive manner by the barrister who stated that he had obviously supported me all the way through all the previous proceedings and by stating that the pistol was not loaded she inferred that this was what he was doing now, rather than accepting what he was saying because it was the truth. This was rather a serious allegation to make against John who was under oath. He felt aggrieved that she had cast doubt upon his character.

After lunch Cliff presented all the mitigation; my impeccable record as a teacher and exemplary record as a citizen who had never been in trouble with the Police before. The psychiatric report was referred to which stated that I was suffering from a condition of anxiety. The forensic psychiatric report commissioned by the DfES confirmed that I am no longer suffering from that condition. The barrister for the GTC then presented her summing up of the case against me. She relied upon that my actions on the night of the incident were as conveyed by Recorder Browne's judgement and I was pleased that I had pointed out the errors in this judgement right at the onset of the hearing. She advocated that my actions had brought the profession into disrepute and had adversely affected public confidence in the profession; both these things could be used to bring the most serious sanction of prohibition against me which would prohibit me from teaching children by removing my registration as a teacher.

Cliff had the final word. He claimed that I had been significantly punished already having been to prison and having lost my job. He argued that the criterion for the lowest sanction of the four levels of sanction were the most appropriate one in this case. All of these criteria such as for example, acting under duress and previous good history, applied to me with possibly one exception- that being 'not deliberate'. He then went on to make the point that because I was in such a state of distress and was later diagnosed as suffering from anxiety my culpability was lowered. He made reference to the judgement of Lord Justice Rose, who stated that my 'culpability had been reduced' and I was not as responsible for my actions as I would have been under normal circumstances. We then retired to allow the panel to consider their decision on sanction or not and if so which one.

It was quite late in the afternoon now being 4.15. The GTC normally finishes its working day at 5 p.m. but can go on until 5.30 in exceptional cases. We sat and waited. Our turn was over there was nothing else we could do except to try to relax. I didn't want to have my registration removed, it would be the final humiliation and would add credibility the convictions, whereas to retain my teaching registration would undermine them. How could I remain a teacher with such serious convictions for gun crime and affray? This is what I worried about as we waited for the verdict.

It turned 5 p.m. and Cliff had missed his train home which was at six minutes past five. The station was right adjacent to the building and he had hoped he may make it. Sue talked about a friend of hers in South Africa who was a barrister. I said she should have brought him with her he might have been better than Cliff and we laughed. Cliff joined us as he realised I was joking. He had been pretty magnificent actually and I was very grateful to him whatever the outcome. Cliff said they may now inform us by letter when it got to 5.30, thinking we would have to leave then. A GTC officer came to tell us they were staying because it wouldn't be long now. I went out to the loo and saw them deliberating through the window in the door. Cliff said they must have reached a decision what would now be taking time was writing up their reasons. They had to present their reasons orally with the decision. Cliff began to worry he may miss his next train an hour later. Then we were called in.

I looked at their faces and they all made good eye contact which I thought was a positive sign. The chairperson Doctor Nadine Bristow said firstly they had deliberated on the issue of the pellets and concluded that on the balance of probabilities they believed that the air pistol was loaded. We were one down. I had always thought however that if it had been loaded it was conclusive proof that I never intended to hurt anyone. If it wasn't loaded I could have been actually trying to shoot the youths but missing. Then she moved on to the sanction stating they thought it was appropriate that a sanction should be imposed. That sanction was a reprimand. This was the lowest sanction, tantamount to a telling off. I was really pleased. I didn't feel vindicated but I did feel I now had some credibility again. The panel had risked public criticism to impose the lowest sanction against me and I was grateful. She went on to give the reasons they thought this sanction was appropriate: she said I had shown insight into my behaviour and remorse, that it was an isolated incident when I was under considerable pressure and that the risk of me repeating the behaviour was low. Also that I appeared to have learned my lesson and the committee had taken into account: my previous employment history, and that my testimonial evidence was highly complimentary, and I had demonstrated a considerable commitment to teaching.

Finally efforts to paint me as a dangerous criminal had failed! A reprimand stays on my record for two years and I must declare it to an employer enquiring about my registration, but after two years it expires. My character referees had done me proud. I think the panel had been somewhat overwhelmed by the quantity and quality of personal support which I had. When I later telephoned Kath, my ex-boss to tell her she said "Well it was all true Linda!" I was most grateful to all of them.

38   Elation and Gratitude

The press were very interested and the media attention was snowballing as we left the GTC, but we wanted to get on our way home first and find somewhere to have a nice meal to celebrate and thank two of my guardian angels, Sue and Nigel. As we sat in the pub I didn't drink much of the wine that we had ordered I felt I would just fall asleep if I did. Sue and Nigel had a good drink I think they were unwinding after all the tension we had been through. Needless to say Sue never stopped talking as John drove us home, as she does when she's had a few! It was lovely.

It was the outrage of the public at my plight that had initially attracted the media attention. Without that I don't believe that any of my prolific complaining would have come to anything, it empowered me. The next day, Wednesday, I was contacted by numerous television programmes, more so than newspapers and radio. I suppose people wanted to actually see the person to be able to judge for themselves. I wanted to do them all. I had not been able to have my say when I came out of prison for fear of jeopardising my job and because I had signed an exclusive contract with the Mail on Sunday. My friends said that was the worse thing I could have done because it effectively gagged me, but it had meant that I was now £25,000 less in debt than I would otherwise have been. Now I could speak to all of them. I didn't want any fee because that would have meant I was restricted. I wanted to let as many of the Great British public as possible know just how much their support had meant to me, how grateful I was to them and how they had saved me from despair. I wanted to thank them from the bottom of my heart and let them know just how humble it had made me feel. The reaction that I got back from people was fantastic, people were so happy for me, really genuinely pleased. I was so pleased that they were pleased because it would have meant nothing without that.

I did BBC Breakfast TV on the Thursday morning, having travelled down to London on Wednesday evening. Whilst at Euston Station waiting to go home I was contacted by GMTV Breakfast TV who wanted me the next day. I said I would come back but I had to go back to Manchester because I had a cookery class that evening and I did not want to let my students or the college down. Richard & Judy wanted me that afternoon, but obviously I could not manage that unfortunately. When I arrived at Manchester Michelle Pontin from Key103 local radio met me and interviewed me outside Piccadilly station. From there I got a taxi to Granada and did Granada Reports and then the ITN News team took me home and interviewed me at our house.

As they left at 4 p.m. I was getting my demonstration ingredients ready for my cookery class when BBC Northwest Tonight rang and wanted me to come to the studio. I had to refuse but they met me in Swinton and interviewed me on the street before I went into my class. As yet again I thanked the public and tried to explain just how much their support had meant a woman stood and watched. When the interview was over she came over to introduce herself, she was one of my ex-students and we hugged and kissed and cried together. It was all so overwhelming and I can't convey sufficiently the gratitude and the feeling of privilege that it gives to me, a warm secure and safe feeling like having a very large loving family. The camera crew were still there, I said to them "this is how people react to me, they are so lovely," they seem to instinctively understand. After my class I got home at ten and at 10.45 a car came to take me back to London to do GMTV in the morning. I got to bed at 2.30 a.m. and had booked a wake up call for 4.30.

I was getting quite tired by now but I knew next week would be too late and if I wanted to get my message across I would have to do it now. In all my interviews I made sure I expressed my thanks to the public. I said I was sorry and ashamed for what I had done. I urged that more be done by the police to tackle anti-social behaviour, saying that although it was low level and low priority crime it did not feel like that when it was aimed at you. I also said that I would not do it again, but now know what I would do. They were interested to hear that besides all the security that we have such as security lighting and lockable gate etc I would if I felt I was being targeted install cameras and even have security to patrol my house. I said people may think this was over the top and too expensive but I pointed out that I had lost my job three years ago and I had earned 30k a year, so could people really afford not to take these steps to protect themselves.

I said that if victims could gather evidence and find out who was responsible they could confront the Police with it. I urged people to keep a log and to report every incident so that the police were aware and could not deny that it was happening. I urged people to complain and be assertive and, rather than just accepting a crime reference number, try to force them to take action. I said next time I would go out with a camera or a video so I had evidence, but I know people have been seriously injured doing this or even accused of perversions. The advice seemed to go down well people seemed to be interested to know how I would tackle it differently with the benefit of hindsight. One thing is for sure I would now make it my priority, I would not bury my head in the sand and hope that it would stop and it would go away and keep trying to get on with my life. Apparently the item after me on the Northwest Tonight programme was about a policeman who had left the force. The reasons he cited for his departure were his frustration with, 'targets, paperwork and the easy collar,' which I thought was quite ironic. I had made the point on Breakfast TV that if I had not been honest and not admitted everything as I had, if I had dropped my air pistol down the grid and denied that I carried one, it would have been a lot more difficult for the DS to have made a case against me. Going for the 'easy target' is a despicable and cowardly practice and it undermines the valuable job that our emergency serivces do.

The following weekend I was told by friends that Alan Beswick of BBC, GMR radio had done another programme on me, a phone in on the subject of, 'Would you let Linda teach your kids?' He had previously done, 'What sentence should Linda get?' after I was convicted when people had rang in with all sorts of weird and wonderful answers like, a medal, a free holiday and target practice! This was when he had interviewed the investigating DS. I decided that I would ring him, now I was free to do so, so on Monday morning I did. The Gary Newlove murderers had just been sentenced that morning. Alan welcomed me onto the show and explained that people had overwhelmingly supported my return to teaching last week with well over 90odd percent saying things like not only would they let me teach their children but they would move them to where I was! It would seem they saw me as some sort of national hero, which was very flattering even if it was undeserved.

I explained that the purpose of my coming on the show was to express my gratitude for all the support and to let people know just how much it had meant to me. I explained that I could not come on last time to comment for fear of it adversely affecting my sentence or jeopardising the hearing for my job but that I had listened and I had found the comments very comforting. He as Granada Reports compared my case and my situation to that of Gary Newlove, the dad from Warrington who had gone out to yobs and been kicked to death. I said that people had said that that could have happened to me. I had no idea who I was going out to. I was asked to comment on their sentence, 17 years for the ringleader. I said I thought they would get about 20 years, they had committed murder so I was not surprised. I told Alan that when he did the first show I was so distressed that I had taken a tranquilizer prescribed by the doctor but following his show I was OK. I know I keep saying it but it saved me, the attitudes expressed and the understanding shown pulled me through, changed my priorities on life and made me strong.

I don't know what else to do now other than to write it down and hope that they/you appreciate one tiny little percent of how much your empathy for me really meant, it meant the world to me!

Thank you from the bottom of my heart.

What about the future? God knows! Enjoying the grandchildren I hope.

Postscript

At the end of July 2008 GMP appointed a new Chief Constable, following the untimely death of Michael Todd, he takes up his position on 1st September 2008. The new head is Peter Fahy previously Chief Constable of the Cheshire Constabulary. Whilst head of Cheshire Police incidents involving nuisance youths and anti-social behaviour have been upgraded in priority, and the response time has been reduced to twenty-five minutes.

In June 2008 Mr Fahy joined a rebellion of senior officers against Home Office targets, claiming they were stifling the police service. It is heartening that he criticised the culture of target-driven policing 'that gives criminal records for playground fights', and said his officers had moved towards common-sense policing, concentrating on bringing to justice real offenders.